MW00777836

SURVIVING....

in spite of everything

A postwar history of the hardware industry

© 2010 Bob Vereen
All Rights Reserved.

No part of this publication may be reproduced, stored in a retrieval system, or transmitted, in any form or by any means, electronic, mechanical, photocopying, recording, or otherwise, without the written permission of the author.

First published by Dog Ear Publishing
4010 W. 86th Street, Ste H
Indianapolis, IN 46268
www.dogearpublishing.net

ISBN: 978-160844-416-8

This book is printed on acid-free paper.

Printed in the United States of America

Acknowledgments

I've read Acknowledgments in other books from time to time, and never realized how much those named people might have helped the author. Now I know.

Tom Delph, John Hammond and Dick Wright, three former co-workers at the National Retail Hardware Association (now *North American Retail Hardware Association*), helped me greatly, reading my preliminary drafts, suggesting things to add, people to mention, and reminding me of events that had a significant impact on the hardware industry. I'm deeply indebted to them.

Don Wolf, an old friend who ran one of the largest firms in the business, and Bob Glennon, another author and a relatively new friend, encouraged me to write this book.

Most of all, however, I want to acknowledge the men and women whom I met in this industry since I first entered it way back in 1950. What a wonderful industry, filled with wonderful people.

May it and they survive forever!

Chapter One

AN INTRODUCTION TO SIX DECADES OF HISTORY

What is it about the hardware industry that has allowed so many of its wholesalers and retailers to survive the postwar period, when up and down the Main Streets of America, virtually all of the independent drug stores, variety stores, office supply stores, clothing stores and shoe stores have disappeared?

Is it because none of those channels of distribution had as many charismatic and visionary leaders as the hardware industry? Or is it because hardware retailers and wholesalers are just tough, adaptable individuals who refuse to give up?

There's no doubt that the ranks of independent hardware and lumberyard retailers are thinned, and the number of full-line hardware wholesalers has dropped dramatically in the last 60 years, but there still are tens of thousands of retailers and nearly 100 full-line wholesalers remaining, most of them far bigger, stronger and tougher than ever and quite determined to continue providing products and services to the American public and American businesses.

Certainly any look back at the postwar years of America's hardware industry is filled with examples of dynamic, dedicated individuals who helped retailers meet the challenges of the times, who provided the guidance and vision which enabled them to become more efficient and productive, who improved the concept of dealer-owned wholesaling or who banded wholesalers together to improve their buying power and strengthen their store-identity marketing efforts by creating store names and programs that implied these individual retailers were part of a larger organization.

They turned tens of thousands of individual retailers into a cohesive industry, one that adjusted to the competitive threats of multi-billion dollar corporate giants. . . who even learned to live with gigantic home centers and other big-box competitors like Walmart and Kmart. . . who fought off a once-powerful Sears and its powerful and respected Craftsman, Weather-beater and other hardlines brands. Their efforts and those of their successors are ongoing. The battle continues.

Some hardware and lumberyard retailers continue to go out of business, of course, but others continue to grow and open additional stores. New entrants into the business are bringing new life and enthusiasm into the hardware industry, one of the oldest retailing fields, one that helped build America and which continues to help build it.

The hardware industry always depended a great deal on the vision, the wisdom and the determination of a few individuals as it met earlier challenges—people like E. C. Simmons of St. Louis, who pioneered store identity programs before the industry was really ready for them. But he helped pave the way. In the postwar period, the industry continues that dependency on the vision, wisdom and leadership of key individuals.

People like Russ Mueller, who re-energized the National Retail Hardware Association into a dynamic marketing entity that coordinated and educated all levels of the industry. . . on individuals like Dick Hesse, Arnold Gerberding and Don Wolf, and John Cotter, who galvanized dealer-ownership into a powerful marketing force, not simply another way of wholesaling. . . of wholesalers like Joe Orgill, Paul Cosgrave, Norm Luekens, John Wallace and Charlie Hildreth, Jr. and many others who provided retailers with systems and store programs, not just merchandise. . . of Bill Davidson, Al Doody and Bert McCammon of Management Horizons, who taught wholesalers, retailers and manufacturers the benefits of professional management and the need to improve inventory turnover via Gross Margin Return on Inventory (GMROI). . . of men like Bernie Marcus and Arthur Blank, who transformed the home center industry with a warehouse format and created a new kind of hardware retailer that changed retailing not only in the United States but around the world.

There are hundreds of other influential men and women who've helped retailers and wholesalers not only survive but thrive since the end of World War II, and this brief history of the industry will cite more of them and discuss some of their accomplishments—but it simply cannot mention all of the influential individuals of the postwar years. There simply are too many who have shaped the industry and enabled it to survive.

Unfortunately for store owners in other retail fields, charismatic, dynamic, wise leaders like these apparently were lacking. That's why, to a very large extent, drug retailing today is dominated by two chains, Walgreens and CVS Caremark. . . why locally owned or franchised variety stores no longer dot Main Street or suburban shopping centers. . . why small town department stores have disappeared.

The only retail field that has survived, similar to hardware, is the local grocer, and for many of the same reasons—the support, vision and guidance of powerful wholesalers—-either corporate or dealer-owned, which provide low cost distribution, marketing support and managerial assistance and education—as well as product.

The postwar years have seen the emergence of powerful retailing chains in every field, including the hardware industry. It witnessed the birth of the most powerful retailer in all the world—Walmart, and the development of discount (or big-box) retailing in all its variations. They spawned the creation of big-box specialty chains like Hobby Lobby, Best Buy, Dick's Sporting Goods, Bed, Bath & Beyond, Office Depot, Staples and Michaels. And a number of others.

The postwar years also have seen virtually every kind of retailer begin stocking some of the merchandise lines considered basic for hardware retailers and lumberyards. Everybody wants to get into the act.

Today, in supermarkets, drug stores, mass merchants and even convenience stores, consumers can buy flashlight batteries, light bulbs, small hand tools, glues, and dozens—if not hundreds—of other basic items hardware retailers rely on somewhat as the foundation of their businesses. The industry's retailers learned to cope with the loss of some of those impulse sales to other channels of trade and, instead, are continuing to develop niches that make them an indispensable and sometimes fascinating part of their local communities and neighborhoods.

This small town Ohio store is a multi-million dollar retailer, including its web site sales and an amazing inventory of non-electric products for its Amish customers.

In the postwar years, hardware stores and, to a lesser extent, lumberyards, have evolved in so many other ways.

When World War II ended, America needed new homes for the new families being created by returning servicemen, and hardware retailers stepped up. They carried major appliances so those new homes could be supplied and the housewares that new wives would be desiring; they stocked the tools with which to build those new homes or to keep them in repair; they carried the paint with which to decorate them; they carried the shovels, seeds and wheelbarrows needed to establish lush new lawns.

And the local lumberyards provided the building materials that were needed to build them, to expand them or to renovate older ones taken over by new owners.

When you needed a hammer or a wrench, you went to the local hardware store. When you needed lumber or bricks or drywall, you went to the local lumberyard.

There were no home centers. . . .no mass merchants. . . and not really very many specialty stores carrying paint or tiles or floor covering.   Yes, there was one giant who stocked those things—and more, and its name was Sears, Roebuck, and there was another smaller but similar chain as a competitor—Montgomery Ward.   But they weren't "everywhere."

There was no interstate highway system for years, so most shopping was local. As a consumer, you went to the local merchant on Main Street, and later, maybe, to the little strip shopping center that had opened on the edge of town. Later still, you might go to the big shopping mall on the outskirts of the nearest metropolitan city for clothing or shoes and maybe to shop the new Sears store there.

Hundreds of relatively small, full line wholesalers provided retailers with the tens of thousands of items hardware stores carried. Transportation limitations restricted many of them to servicing dealers within a radius of a few hundred miles, typically. Many of those wholesalers had once been successful retailers who wanted to grow, and thus became wholesalers.

Thousands of returning servicemen and women, coming back from the war, decided to become retailers and opened hardware stores and lumberyards to serve their communities, or bought out existing stores to inject new life into old retailing entities.

Life was much simpler in those days. As a retailer, you bought from a local wholesaler. His salesman (or rarely, a saleswoman) called on you weekly or every other week and checked your "want book" to see what you needed, suggested one or two new things the company had acquired and maybe showed you some samples he was carrying, and the merchandise you ordered was delivered in a week or so.

Your wholesaler salesman carried a huge catalog and you and he (or she) reviewed it to see if there was anything else you needed. Sometimes, your wholesaler supplied you with a copy of its catalog so you had a ready reference for future and "special" ordering and for answering customer queries.

Your merchandise, by and large, was not packaged. Paint came in cans, of course, and some items were boxed, but very little attention was paid to using those containers to help sell the product by talking about user benefits, installation techniques or providing other self-help information.

In fact, you realized that you did more than sell products. You dispensed advice every day.

You opened the store Monday through Saturday, but you closed by 5 or 6 pm. You didn't stay open every night. In some towns, you might stay open till 8 or 9 pm one night when the whole town stayed open. You never opened on Sunday, unless a good customer called you in a panic with a problem and a need for some of your products.

Your customers included the tradesmen and contractors in your local town or trading area, along with those consumers who felt comfortable in painting their homes or fixing things that might need fixing. You attracted hunters and fishermen with your sporting goods, housewives with your housewares and gift sections, and at Christmas time, you were toy head-quarters for your town or area. You also supplied fellow businessmen and women with the products they needed to keep their stores, factories and warehouses in good shape. Plus local farmers who were, by necessity, jacks-of-all trades and needed lots of things from their local hardware merchant. Indeed, they were the original Do-It-Yourselfers.

You stocked housewares because you wanted to be a one-stop destination for the families in your area, and you carried a better quality range than did the local variety store. As small electric appliances began to be invented, you added them, too.

You were the headquarters for sporting goods, supplying the hunters and fishermen with the supplies they needed—or simply lusted for. You also were the toy headquarters in your town, in many cases, when Christmas rolled around.

You might run a small ad occasionally in your local newspaper, but you really weren't a very big advertiser because you didn't have to be. Everybody knew where you were, knew what you carried, and knew their only other choices were to shop another hardware store or lumberyard in your town. Or drive to another city or town. In many towns and cities, you were active civically and sometimes even politically.

Your store wasn't very big; your merchandise was only loosely arranged by department; it was displayed on flat tables or maybe those new-fangled tiered tables being sold and installed by your local hardware association; you didn't worry as much about shoplifting; your employees were almost always full-time and were with you for years so they knew products about as well as you did. You probably hadn't had any retail training. You either grew up in a hardware family or felt you knew how to use all the kinds of products you sold so you decided running a hardware store made sense for you. In other words, in most cases, you were not a "professional retailer."

The local lumberyard wasn't much of a competitor. Its sales floor was really just a fairly small office. It carried a handful of tools and just a smattering of other items you might stock. Its own product range was stored in a big outdoor facility and a few covered buildings.

And yet, you thrived. You met the needs of your community. You were one of the mainstays of Main Street.

And then, things began to change.

Chapter Two

THE BEGINNING OF RETAIL CHANGES

Retailing of any kind is a never-ending series of changes, depending on competition, economics, climate, the dynamics of companies, and, increasingly of late, technological changes . . . in addition to the drive and charisma of individuals with their dreams and new ideas.

Hardware retailing is no different, nor has it been in the postwar years.

In the postwar hardware industry, as the pent-up demand for new homes developed, retailing began to change in numerous ways. More stores opened as returning vets became retailers. Existing retailers sold out or turned their businesses over to the next generation and these new, younger owners in many cases brought fresh ideas and a more aggressive attitude. The population explosion created new families and the need for new housing. It also attracted competition. Other kinds of retailers soon decided they too wanted to cash in on the booming construction business.

The suburbs began developing, as did suburban shopping. Strip centers, then enclosed malls.

Wholesalers began to expand their territories as roads and transportation improved. The small, local wholesaler began finding it harder to compete as larger wholesalers with more capital began offering more services and products and began encouraging retailers to "join a group". The "personal relationship" between wholesale salesman and the retailer sometimes was the only thing keeping some small, local wholesalers in business.

But large or small, wholesalers were working hard to find ways to develop dealer loyalty and get dealers to concentrate more of their purchases instead of spreading their buying among a number of distributors. Early attempts at bringing retailers under a common promotional umbrella began to be successful.

Earlier efforts, some long before the war, had not been very successful as independent retailers demonstrated their staunch independence by rejecting most such efforts, plus chain stores were not as successful or as important as competitors in the prewar days so independent retailers felt no need to seek the greater prominence of a merchandising/promotional group. Independent retailers could afford to be independent. Sears, and to a lesser extent, Montgomery Ward, were the only really strong chain competitors most hardware and lumber/building material retailers contended with, although some franchise organizations, like those mentioned below, brought competitive retailing to many American Midwestern communities.

Up in Minneapolis, Minnesota, two companies, which had been in operation even before the war, recognized the postwar opportunity and took immediate steps to grow at a faster pace in the immediate postwar years. They aggressively recruited new people into the industry and opened new retail outlets across the Midwest heartland.

Bert Gamble and Phil Skogmo had formed their company, Gamble-Skogmo, before the war to establish in the Upper Midwest's small towns a Main Street merchant that would compete, to some degree, with local hardware stores by selling some hardware, paint, and other fix-up products, but base their main appeal on an extensive assortment of automotive products and because of their location, a heavy emphasis on sporting goods. Gamble stores also heavily promoted toys in season. Gamble stores competed with independent hardware retailers by offering a more modern sales floor, a somewhat different merchandise assortment, a fairly extensive array of private branded merchandise, more competitive prices and aggressive direct mail advertising.

A Gamble store did not duplicate the typical hardware store's broad assortment of fix-up products, but would offer the basics, plus automotive items such as tires, car-care equipment and other items hardware stores typically didn't carry. It would carry enough hardware-store items to siphon off some sales and be something of a one-stop source for farmers, ranchers, automobile owners and home owners. In some ways—although much smaller physically, it might have been the predecessor of today's farm/fleet stores such as Tractor Supply.

Gamble-Skogmo stores were both company-owned as well as franchised. Gamble officials guided franchisees on inventory assortment, provided advertising assistance and designed the stores for them. At its peak, Gamble-Skogmo was a relatively huge multi-million dollar company serving hundreds of retailers when even the largest conventional hardware wholesaler did far less in sales.

Right after the war, it held a gigantic buying/merchandising/planning show and meeting in Minneapolis called the Gamble Plan-o-Rama, in which hundreds of existing and potential Gamble dealers came to see new merchandise being made available now that the war had ended and to learn of Gamble's plans for aggressive expansion. It was the forerunner of the buying/merchandising shows and markets so common now and conducted by both privately owned and dealer-owned wholesalers.

Across town in Minneapolis, another franchise operation also was thriving in the postwar years. Started in 1928 by Arthur, Maurice and Louis Melamed, Coast to Coast was similar to Gamble stores in one way, but with a greater emphasis on hardware kinds of products, plus some housewares. Like Gamble stores, because of their location, they also carried sporting goods and, in season, promoted toys. It was a complete franchise and, like Gambles, had begun prewar but reached its peak in the immediate postwar years. At its peak, there were about 1,200 Coast to Coast dealers scattered over 26 states.

Coast to Coast stores were common in Upper Midwest states and even found their way as far west as the Pacific Coast and as far east as Ohio. Coast stores were not large—about the size of a typical hardware store at the time. What made them different was that inventory was determined by its buyers in the head office. Other factors which distinguished a Coast to Coast store from a typical hardware retailer of its time were the planned store layout, standard fixtures and that there was little, if any, product duplication.

Coast buyers determined the brands—for hammers, saws, electrical fittings, pots and pans, etc. The goal was higher turnover than that enjoyed by the typical small town merchant who duplicated so many brands and items, plus the home office provided ongoing product education and other operational assistance. Coast offered 23,000 stock-keeping units in 12 merchandising departments. It wasn't a "cherry-picking" assortment, by any means.

Store owners came to buying shows once or twice a year, where they attended product knowledge sessions and had a chance to go from booth to booth checking over "show specials".

Store layout was controlled by the home office. Advertising was supplied by the home office, too, and consisted of circulars and catalogs for key seasons such as Christmas. Coast stores were, for many years, much more regular advertisers than the average hardware store. Coast to Coast sought investors and set them up as new retailers, providing everything they needed to become Main Street merchants.

Coast to Coast and Gamble stores were "chains" in everything but ownership.

In the early postwar years, both groups succeeded, but as the years went on, other retailing developments and ownership transitions ultimately marked their end. Both firms were dependent on the drive and vision of their founders—Gamble and Skogmo in one instance and the Melamed brothers for Coast to Coast. Phil Skogmo died before Gamble, and then Bert Gamble began to look beyond his retailing activities to build a larger empire—acquiring a major investment company, as one example. He no longer focused his energies and vision entirely on the retail/wholesale business. The business ultimately was sold and, under new and less dedicated management, failed to change as needed in the ever-changing retail environment and ultimately closed down. Its retail format simply became less effective.

Something similar happened at Coast to Coast. As the Melameds reached retirement age, they decided to sell out in 1962 to Household Finance Corp., a major investment house at the time. Some of the magic went out of Coast to Coast with the sale. The Melamed charisma was gone.

Under President Roger Stangeland, a long time Coast employee, Coast to Coast did much to keep up with the times. It encouraged existing stores to expand and opened larger new stores to compete. Some Coast dealers did as much as $1 million annually, a far cry from the small stores originally founded. It even opened a few home centers. Coast dealers, however, didn't maintain the loyalty to the company they had under its founders and at the same time, conventional hardware wholesalers were offering other items and brands and sometimes lower prices to them than the tightly controlled Coast offerings. Individual hardware retailers also were becoming more aggressive advertisers, were sprucing up their stores and generally being a far more effective competitor. Coast stores, many remaining quite small, became less attractive to consumers.

The company eventually was sold to ServiStar, a dealer-owned wholesaler in Butler, PA, and eventually Coast stores disappeared entirely from the American retailing scene.

Minnesota, for a state without a huge population, was the birthplace of a surprising number of larger wholesalers. One reason was it was the most densely populated state until one hit the West Coast and it was the transportation hub—the kickoff point— into the Dakotas and Montana.

In addition to Gambles and Coast to Coast, there were Our Own Hardware, Farwell, Ozmun, Kirk & Co. and some smaller Twin City firms, plus Marshall Wells and Kelley How Thompson (both from Duluth). United Hardware of Minneapolis ,a dealer-owned wholesaler founded after World War II, has survived when some other dealer-owned firms did not, including Our Own Hardware, one of the two oldest dealer-owned firms. Indeed, United is the only surviving Minnesota wholesaler.

Coast to Coast and Gambles weren't the only identified retailers in the early postwar period or the only ones offering a lot of car care items, which traditional hardware stores were not featuring. Western Auto, headquartered in Kansas City, was another similar group, and there were other regional firms like them elsewhere in the U. S. White's Auto Stores in the southwest was another such company. None carried as many plumbing, paint or electrical items as did a typical hardware store, but all carried hand tools, spray paints, generally some sporting goods, toys in season—enough to be a competitor to some degree for Main Street merchants. Like Coast to Coast and Gambles, the layouts and merchandise assortments of these stores were primarily directed from corporate headquarters.

Variety chains were prevalent in the immediate postwar period and, to some extent, provided some competition to traditional hardware retailers, though the product quality of items they stocked and the price points were usually much lower, but they did siphon off some business. Woolworths and Kresge were the two biggest chains, but there were others like Murphy, T. G. & Y. and a number of others.

Stores like this were to be found on Main Streets and town squares all across America.

Of course, conventional wholesalers always had helped eager would-be retailers get into the business by selling them opening stocks. The local wholesale salesman generally sat down with a prospective dealer and helped him determine his opening stock. Wholesalers often gave extended dating to these neophyte owners, particularly if they did not have a good customer in the trading area already. New store openings gave them wedges into new markets.

It was only later in the postwar period that these efforts began to be more organized, similar to those of Gambles and Coast to Coast, with wholesalers providing guidance on store locations, store sizes, store layout and design and better researched information on basic inventories.

Other changes were taking place elsewhere in America. In some metro areas, larger retailers were being developed which included lumber and building materials in their merchandise mix. Some began as hardware stores adding those products; others began as lumberyards that decided to go more aggressively after consumer business so they added full lines of hardware, expanded tools, added paint, electrical products, etc. They were aggressive entrepreneurs who recognized the opportunities in postwar America, hungry for new homes or to refurbish and expand existing homes. More than many traditional hardware retailers, they seized the opportunity and began expanding store sizes as well as their marketing efforts and their inventories.

These became the original pioneer home centers—firms like Central Hardware of St. Louis, Ernst in the state of Washington, Forest City in Cleveland, Lindsley Lumber down in Florida and Grossmans in Massachusetts. Handyman in San Diego. Hechingers, based in Washington, DC. There'll be more about these stores in the Big-box/Home Centers chapter.

Meanwhile, local lumberyards began courting more consumer business as well, and kept adding more shelf goods to their inventories. Some decided that the little sales offices they maintained simply weren't big enough and developed regular sales floors, most not as big as a normal hardware store but much larger than they had had previously.

Retailers who had always concentrated on buying—of determining their personal choice of brands and products from a variety of wholesalers—were beginning to realize they might be smarter to leave at least some of the buying decisions to one or two of their major wholesalers and to become a more aggressive and effective selling organization. Obviously, wholesalers worked hard to encourage this trend. This didn't mean that retailers delegated all buying to their primary wholesaler. That simply wasn't—and isn't—the independent hardware retailer's way of operating. They still found it smart to "personalize" their assortments, to develop niche departments, to emphasize categories that no other retailer in their trading area was stocking or promoting. This also gave them the opportunity to sell a lot of merchandise that he or she personally liked. It's hard to beat owner-enthusiasm for categories and products.

Independent hardware stores continued to change physically, too. State and regional hardware associations were offering store remodeling and expansion services, as did some wholesalers—all of them encouraging retailers to modernize their stores, install new gondola shopping fixtures, expand. A great many retailers expanded their stores, moving up from 2,000 sq. ft. or so to 5,000 sq. ft. and even 10,000 sq. ft.

While retail chains were developing in other fields, such as drug stores and supermarkets, the retail hardware industry remained relatively chain-free. True, there were small clusters of stores owned by the same man or family, but they were largely restricted to a very small, local area. One of the few larger chains that grew and grew was the W. E. Aubuchon Co. in New England, which began in Massachusetts, spread into other New England states and finally edged its way into upstate New York. It continues today as a chain of more than 120 stores.

Another was (and is) Orchard Supply Hardware, now owned by Sears. Originally an orchard owner's cooperative in San Jose, California, it became a local, closely-held corporation with a large main store for its time and then a second store. Under President Al Smith, son of the orchard cooperative's head, and general merchandise manager Ken Lewis, the firm met with such success that it began aggressively opening other stores. Its stores were large for the time—25,000 sq. ft. or more. Today, it not only operates in northern California but also in the Los Angeles area. It underwent several ownership changes over the years before being acquired by Sears.

Still another regional chain is Westlake Ace Hardware, originally headquartered in Moberly, Missouri. A member of Ace Hardware even before Ace became a cooperative, Westlake has grown steadily over the years and today operates stores in several Midwestern states. Its stores are larger than the typical independent hardware store or the Aubuchon chain, though not as large as those of Orchard Supply Hardware on the West Coast.

Still another chain is Aco Hardware, which operates in the Detroit suburban area. Founded by Ted Traskos, it originally belonged to the Ace organization, but as it began expanding and encroaching on other Ace stores, it had to change its name or limit its expansion. It made a one-letter change and also began to do its own distribution, setting up its own large warehouse distribution center.

Interestingly, however, quite a few more chains developed in the lumber/building material business, some growing from small regional chains into larger ones and some even becoming national in size and scope.

Although the industry lacked any truly large regional chains, wholesalers began uniting independent retailers under a number of common names to simulate the supposed buying efficiencies and lower pricing of the chain stores prevalent in other categories. Some of the earlier proponents of this marketing strategy were the dealer-owned wholesalers such as Our Own Hardware in Minneapolis and American Hardware Supply Co., originally based in Pittsburgh. Ace Hardware out of Chicago was not a cooperative originally, but dealers affiliated with it identified their individually owned stores as Jones Ace Hardware or, often, simply as Ace Hardware. Another was the Marshall Wells Co., a wholesaler based in Duluth, Minnesota. Its Marshall Wells-identified stores were, at one time, quite successful in several Upper Midwest states.

Thousands of retailers now use various program names as their identity, with or without their own names.

Hibbard, Spencer, Bartlett Co., a large wholesaler located outside Chicago, banded its dealers together under the True Value name. Hibbard was one of the early and successful wholesalers with a program name that meant something to the consumer, but ownership missteps and other problems began plaguing the company and it finally went bankrupt. However, the True Value name was then acquired by Cotter & Co., a dealer-owned cooperative. In the process, John Cotter also acquired several key executives who went on to be important leaders in the industry. This turned out to be a pattern for Cotter and helped fuel his firm's amazing growth. When old-line wholesalers closed, he recruited key individuals from them, who helped him sign up customers of the closing (or closed) wholesale firm.

Soon other wholesalers joined in the store-identity game, either as individual wholesalers or as members of buying/merchandising groups. Other dealer-owneds also began emphasizing a common store identity. Over the years, especially as time passed, consumers began to read and hear about True Value stores, (then under the direction of Cotter & Co., which is now known as True Value Hardware), Trustworthy stores, Sentry stores, Pro Hardware stores, Do It Best stores under the Hardware Wholesalers, Inc. banner. That firm later changed its own name to Do It Best.

Pro Hardware, founded by Paul Cosgrave, an ex employee with Minnesota's Janney, Semple, Hill & Co., brought together non-competitive wholesalers from around the country and provided them with promotional material, central buying and a unifying store program name, Pro Hardware.

Wholesalers encouraged retailers to adopt common store layouts and to integrate the store identity with their own names (i.e., Smith Ace Hardware) or simply, Pro Hardware, if there was no other Pro-affiliated retailer in their trading area.

They were bound together by their common names and the advertising efforts organized by their wholesalers, with True Value, the name promoted by dealer-owned Cotter & Co. (now True Value Hardware) probably the most aggressively promoted in the early stages. Cotter & Co. used direct mail circulars and catalogs, as well as radio and television. Its efforts were largely based on advertising money contributed by manufacturers, due to the extensive prodding of Edward Lanctot, Cotter & Co.'s general merchandise manager, who was, by all odds, the most aggressive merchandiser and marketer among wholesalers in his time.

All these store programs had one goal—to convince the American consumer that the local identified store had the best prices, the best quality and the best service.

That this strategy was and is effective is borne out by the fact that Ace Hardware, now a dealer-owned firm of some 4,000+ stores, has been winning awards for having the best customer service in the hardware/home center industry, as though it were a corporate chain like Sears, Home Depot or Lowe's.

Wholesalers were helping in other ways, too, by encouraging retailers to add new lines and helping their customers promote these new lines as well as their basic products, and by improving and expanding the direct mail advertising they had offered for years. From once or twice a year promotions, advertising became more seasonal—spring, summer, fall and Christmas. In addition to circulars, catalogs began to be developed in order to present a broader range of products to consumers. Some wholesalers also sponsored group advertising in larger metro areas and a few even ran advertising in national magazines. In some instances, wholesalers offered monthly circulars. And as technology improved, they began offering custom-made circulars to their dealers, especially for events such as new store openings, anniversary sales, etc.

Millions of wholesaler-produced circulars and catalogs help retailers promote their products.

They also developed monthly promotions, calling them by such names as "Bargains of the Month"—special buys on individual items, generally but not always seasonal, that retailers could promote on gondola ends and with window and/or in-store banners and signs, as well as local advertising if they chose. These were—and continue to be—important traffic-builders, supplementing the circulars and catalogs offered by wholesalers.

Toys were, for a number of years, one of the most successful seasonal categories for thousands of retailers, bringing families into hardware stores during the important Christmas season. Ultimately, however, this business was lost to lower-priced mass merchants.

Wholesalers like Supplee-Biddle-Steltz of Philadelphia developed special toy circulars, such as its Billy & Ruth toy book (named for Steltz' two children) and offered them to other wholesalers. These glossy, four-color catalogs presented toys in handsome fashion. By grouping press run quantities, costs were kept low so independent retailers were able to afford them and promoted their assortment in a more impressive fashion than other local merchants. Other wholesalers banded together to produce similar handsome, four-color toy circulars and Christmas catalogs.

It was an exciting time to be a retailer. New families meant new customers. New houses were being built and old ones remodeled and improved, so there was a constant need for the products and services being offered by hardware and lumber retailers. Suburbs were being developed with builders building hundreds of homes at a time.

Hardware stores were uniquely positioned to service these needs. They had the broadest inventories. . . .carried all those odds and ends needed to repair, replace or refinish. . . didn't worry if they carried some items for a long time, just as long as they could supply a customer with what he or she needed when it was needed. Their employees knew their products and were able to provide the advice and counsel customers needed. In other words, they were perfectly situated as the Do It Yourself movement became "officially" recognized.

However, these opportunities did not go unnoticed. Out east, a firm called E. J. Korvette decided to offer a wide range of products, including some of those stocked by hardware stores, at a lower gross margin than other retailers of the time. A few other new "discount" stores emerged and began to be one-stop shops for American consumers.

Up in Michigan, one of the pioneer variety store chains, S. S. Kresge, recognized how America was changing and looked at the few under-financed discounters evolving out East, and decided it needed to develop larger discount stores. Thus was borne Kmart. A department store chain in Minneapolis, The Dayton Co., came to the same conclusion and founded a discount chain called Target. So did Woolworth executives, who set up their own Woolco discount stores.

And down south in Arkansas, a franchised Ben Franklin dealer by the name of Sam Walton looked at his own small town Main Street variety store and thought about how it would be affected—and put out of business—if discounters came his way.

He decided to go East and look them over. He did, and came back with the decision that he'd better close his variety store and open up a larger store, located on the edge of town, and begin selling at lower prices. The rest of that story, as the saying goes, is history.

The last few decades

Hardware stores and lumber/building material dealers, along with the pioneer home center chains, found   themselves facing an even greater threat than Kmart, Target or Woolco and a fast-growing Walmart as the years progressed—the emergence of Home Depot and the resurgence of Lowe's, both of which will be discussed in detail in the following Home Center chapter, along with another amazing retailer, privately-owned Menards, which operates in the Midwest.

Chapter Three

HOME CENTERS AND OTHER BIG-BOXES

Undoubtedly the development of large home improvement stores, later to be called home centers, turned out to be the most momentous change in the hardware industry in the postwar period. It overshadowed everything else.

But before home centers came to be such a dominant competitive factor for the average or typical hardware store or lumber/building material retailer, owners had to learn to cope with another big-box retailer—the discounter or mass merchant. They are still fighting this battle, though against far fewer opponents.

Some might contend that the first "big-boxes" actually were the pioneer home centers, though no one called them that in the early stages. They simply went by their names, such as Forest City Material, Handyman or Central Hardware. They were big city multi-store groups, operating stores of 25,000-50,000 sq. ft., huge for the time when many hardware stores were 2,000-4,000 sq. ft. or so. In addition to basic hardware-store lines, they carried lumber and building materials and, with the space they had, were very strong in seasonal lines such as outdoor living and lawn and garden. They also had enough space to promote décor products and paint by showing miniature room settings. But they affected only the hardware stores and lumberyards in those home cities or maybe a few adjoining suburban towns.

Discounters, however, drew consumers from a much wider area, due to their broader assortments of apparel, footwear, health and beauty aids and housewares, plus modest assortments of hand tools, paint and sundries, extensive lawn and garden merchandise, some plumbing and electrical items (nothing very complicated for consumers to install). They were a one-stop retailer for a whole family's needs. Consumers came from surrounding towns, often driving miles to shop at these new, exciting stores that promoted low prices aggressively and generally offered merchandise at lower cost than traditional merchants of all kinds.

Discounting began along the East Coast in densely populated areas like New York City and northern New Jersey, but quickly was duplicated elsewhere. New England was another area in which early discounting prospered. The pioneer discounters, like E J Korvette and Masters, however, were very thinly capitalized and did not survive, but they did establish an entirely new kind of retailing.

Harry Cunningham of S. S. Kresge Co., in Michigan, is generally considered the first executive of a major company to eagerly adopt the concept. Properly so, he recognized the threat they posed to traditional variety retailing. He established Kmarts—well financed, attractively designed and smartly merchandised and promoted. Much bigger than a Kresge variety store, in suburbia, with their own parking lots. A great draw for the entire family's needs—all at lower retail prices.

The Dayton Co. in Minneapolis, a leading department store, was another established retailer which decided to add a discount division—Target. L. S. Ayres of Indianapolis, still another respected department store chain, began its Ayr-way division. Woolworths established its Woolco units. Other lesser names followed suit. Target survived; Ayres and Ayr-way did not, nor did Woolco and the other lesser names.

It was while all this was going on, in its earliest stages, that Sam Walton decided to ditch his Ben Franklin variety store after going east to look over this new kind of retailer and joined the group, establishing a few of his own discount stores in smaller cities in the South. He called his fledgling company Walmart. The rest is history.

These discounters, or mass merchants as they are now known, sold products in huge quantities and at much lower margins than traditional merchants and soon began putting smaller merchants out of business in many merchandise categories. Many referred to them as "category killers". Of course, as has been documented many times in many places, the weaker discounters did not survive, and today, Walmart is not only the largest mass merchant, it is the world's largest retailer and the world's largest company, employing nearly 2 million people and racking up more than $400 billion in sales. Much of Walmart's current sales are due to its move into food retailing a few years ago, which now makes it America's #1 food retailer.

It operates in a number of international countries as well as with more than 4,000 stores of several types in the United States. Meanwhile, Target, the next largest mass merchandiser, has pared back its hardware-type products dramatically and is far less of a concern to the hardware industry.

Kmart, once the nation's largest discounter but now much weaker, still offers an assortment of hardware-store items comparable to that of Walmart. Its offering is somewhat stronger now than previously because the well known and respected Craftsman products of Sears now are found in Kmart stores as well as Sears, since Kmart now owns Sears. Kmart was purchased by Edward Lampert, an investor, who later bought Sears. Because of his heavy stock-holdings in both companies as "management", he has been closing a number of Sears stores that anchored shopping centers and engineered the addition to Kmart's inventory of Craftsman and some of the other well known Sears private brands.

By putting Sears brands into Kmarts, Lampert has greatly increased its exposure to the public. Sears was operating only about 800 large department stores anchoring malls (before closing some under-performing stores). Adding Sears brands to more than 1,000 Kmart inventories is bound to bring the brand closer to consumers.

Given the lack of sales help in any mass merchandiser, however, one might justifiably wonder if some of the movement off the Kmart shelves of Craftsman products is actually the result of shoplifting, rather than actual sales?

Today Walmart and Kmart do pose a sales concern to competitive hardware and home centers in some merchandise categories. They are particularly strong in lawn and garden, with sizeable outdoor areas devoted to live goods, fertilizers and other lawn-care products.   Both carry some power equipment, too, though they limit their selection to a few models. Target, with its emphasis more on apparel and housewares, generally is not nearly as much of a factor in that category. Many Targets are located in or near strip shopping centers and many have no outside lawn and garden section at all.

Hardware retailers were not isolated from this price-oriented competition, and lost some sales to discounters and continue to do so, but the saving grace for the hardware man (or woman) is the fact that discounters limit their assortments in order to achieve the higher turnover needed to compensate for a lower gross margin and their utter lack of competent sales help on the sales floor to explain products, advise on usage and suggest necessary related items.   In fact, in many cases, it was (and remains) hard to find sales help of any kind.

Convenience undoubtedly is one of the main attractions of one-stop shopping, but the surviving mass merchants are excellent seasonal promoters—lawn and garden, toys, Christmas.

The home center era

Some of the pioneer home centers began as lumberyards, others as hardware stores.   They weren't to be confused with the local hardware chains or lumberyard chains to be found in some cities—not like Warner Hardware, a small chain in Minneapolis long gone, or the still-operating Aco Hardware in the Detroit suburban market, for example, whose stores were smaller and did not contain lumber or building materials.

A group of them, the true pioneers, banded together informally and met once or twice a year to exchange ideas.   They called themselves the MEG Group, standing for Management Exchange Group.
Among the members were these firms (a partial list):

Central Hardware of St. Louis (and later also of Indianapolis and some other cities)
Forest City of Cleveland
Ernst Hardware of Seattle and suburbs
Lindsley Lumber, headquartered in Miami
Grossmans, a Massachusetts-based chain that began as a lumberyard

Hechingers, in the Washington, DC area
J. Pascal, located in Montreal, Canada

They were regular advertisers, often running multi-page newspaper circular inserts weekly when hardware stores rarely advertised. Often buying direct or through feeder wholesalers which gave them special pricing, they created an image of being lower priced than the average hardware store, though their margins were still well into the 30s typically. But the image they wanted they achieved! They also had enough space to mass display some lines such as power lawn mowers, barbecue grills, etc., and those big displays created the impression of hot prices. Also, with the extra space, they were able to create attractive displays which encouraged consumers to remodel, redecorate, expand homes, etc.

The advantage of extra space for mass displays of larger items not only gave these stores the opportunity to display step-up models, it created the impression of low prices based on bulk buying. Extra space also was used to create model rooms, spurring sales of improved bathrooms, kitchens, remodeled and redecorated rooms. Pity the poor husband whose wife studied those displays!

Entrepreneurial retailers, whether hardware retailers or lumbermen, always have been quick to latch onto trends, and as time progressed and home improvement and Do It Yourself became more widespread, many smaller independent stores decided the home center concept made sense for them and thus a lot of individual home centers and small local home center chains also came into being. A classic example is All American Home Center of Downey, California, now a huge store of some 175,000 sq. ft., which, incidentally, now competes with a Home Depot that opened at the edge of its own parking lot a few years back. Talk about nearby competition!

These other smaller home center chains began emerging all around the country—firms like Ole's of Rosemead, California, and Build 'n Save, also in the Los Angeles, Jerry's of Eugene, Oregon; Handyman of Fairborn, Ohio; the Taylor family's group of stores in Virginia Beach, Virginia. Some lumber/building material chains also revamped their stores to go after the consumer business to a greater degree, including some that even became home centers.

But home center retailing is a difficult business, a fact that not everyone recognized at first. As this retailing concept began to capture the public's attention, it also attracted the attention of other businesses.

Walmart, a discounter at the time but nowhere near its giant size of today, decided that it should open some home centers, too. It did open some, about a half dozen at its peak, and soon discovered the problems— finding, hiring and training personnel who could supply answers about products and home improvement projects and the heavy payroll costs this incurred. It also quickly realized that its inventories were broad and expensive and weren't turning at anywhere near the rate inventories were turning in their discount stores. In relatively short order, Walmart's excursion into hardware/home center retailing ended and the stores were closed.

Other giant businesses were intrigued with the home center concept, too. W. R. Grace Co., a large, diversified public company, began acquiring home center chains around the country, and at one time was the largest player in the industry. But returns on investment weren't satisfactory; key people left, and ultimately, Grace was no longer a factor in the industry.

Bowater, a Texas paper company, is another public company that dabbled in home center retailing without making a success of it and it, too, closed up shop.

In the 1960s, Bob Vereen, then editor of HARDWARE RETAILING, and Jerry Hoefferle, head of Build n' Save, decided to start another management-exchange group, similar to the MEG Group. Vereen called it the BIG Group (Better Information Group) and because he knew so many firms around the country, he enlisted quite a number of member firms, while Hoefferle also did some recruiting, bringing in the Ole's firm in particular. The BIG Group, unlike MEG, included some chains that were larger hardware stores, such as Orchard Supply, and later added some lumberyard chains such as Foxworth-Galbraith of Texas.

The years weren't kind to the MEG Group because the rise of Home Depot, heading for the big city markets in which they were dominant, ultimately resulted in the demise of all its members. However, the BIG Group survives, partially because its members serve a number of smaller markets and partially because they've learned how to compete with the two dominant giants, Home Depot and Lowe's.

The years weren't kind to any of the pioneer home centers, whether MEG members or not. Here is a partial list of some of the casualties:

Angels of the Los Angeles area.
Build 'n Save of the Los Angeles area
Builders Emporium, based in Van Nuys, California
Builders Square, based in Texas (later acquired by Kmart)
Central Hardware, based in St. Louis, Mo.
Ernst Home Centers, based in Seattle, Washington
Forest City, based in Cleveland, Ohio
Grossmans, based in Boston, Massachusetts
Handy Andy of Chicago
Handy City out of New Orleans
Handy Dan out of California
Handyman, based in San Diego, California
Hechingers, based in Washington, DC
Home Quarters Warehouse of Virginia
Payless Cashway, based in Kansas City, Missouri
Rickel and Channel, two chains based in New Jersey
Scotty's of Florida
Somerville Lumber, headquartered in Massachusetts

Plus a number of others, many smaller like Clasters of Pennsylvania, Stambaugh-Thompson of Youngstown, Ohio, Courtesy Lumber of suburban Chicago, etc.

Today the BIG Group, unlike MEG, is still in existence and includes some of its original members, but has added new members such as the large Aubuchon hardware chain headquartered in Massachusetts. Vereen retired from managing the group and it is now being managed by Mike McClelland, retired CEO of Do it Best Corp., the big hardware co-op.

In the heady days of the home center industry, home centers helped educate the American public about Do It Yourself. One of the most interesting ways in which they did this was to sponsor gigantic Do It Yourself consumer shows—a combination of a consumer merchandise show and an educational event.

How-to demonstrations in consumer shows like this were very popular for a number of years, conducted by a number of different retailers and attracting tens of thousands of DIYers or potential DIYers.

These events included merchandise displays by hundreds of participating manufacturers, lasted several days, attracted as many as a hundred thousand or more consumers and in demonstration after demonstration educated those consumers on how to repair, replace and repaint anything and everything one would find in an American home or apartment.

Manufacturers, of course, paid for the privilege of exhibiting in the events, but it was a worthwhile expense. Consumers learned how to tackle DIY projects and were encouraged to do them. One of the first (and maybe the very first) to stage such events was the Handyman chain out of San Diego. Soon others followed, and at one time, there were probably half a dozen or more such events taking place around the country.

They continued for a number of years, but finally disappeared, but not before convincing a large number of consumers in major metro markets that DIY was a worthwhile—and doable—activity.

While huge DIY shows are gone, educational efforts continue as hundred or perhaps thousands of individual and chain retailers are now conducting How-to classes and clinics, most often on weekends when consumers can attend.

In 1978, everything changed

The southern California area around Los Angeles spawned quite a number of home center chains, among them a firm called Handy Dan. Its president at one time was a man named Sanford Sigiloff, now best remembered in the industry as the man who fired Bernie Marcus and Arthur Blank, leading them to found Home Depot, along with a third man named Pat Farrah.

Actually, Farrah was the man who conceived the idea of the bare-bones, extremely low-priced home center, and he founded one in the suburban Los Angeles area but it was so under-capitalized that it lasted only a few months.

In 1978, the actions of Marcus, Blank and Farrah changed the industry dramatically.

Marcus and Blank decided that with some refinements, better capitalization and better organization, Farrrah's concept might work, so they teamed up. While he was one of the founding members, Farrah's role never equalled that of Marcus and Blank, and he did not remain with the company, resigning early on and then, many years later, rejoining it again for a short time.

It was Marcus and Blank who built what is now the world's largest home center chain and the model for home center retailing around the world—the warehouse look.

One of their commitments for the future was to treat employees far better than they had been treated, and this philosophy led to employee enthusiasm and initiative which helped the fledgling chain grow at an

*This unusual and attractive Home Depot front was dictated by local regu-
lations in an Illinois community.*

amazing pace. They created a free-wheeling atmosphere at Depot and gave local store managers and merchants a free hand. They credit decentralization for creating Home Depot's vaunted early culture. They recruited tradesmen and other skilled professionals to offer in-store service and rewarded employees with stock. Many became millionaires as the company's stock skyrocketed over the years.

The first 3 Home Depots opened in Atlanta, Georgia, in 60,000 sq. ft. vacated buildings which had previously housed some failed big-box discount units opened by the JC Penney department store chain. The stores generated about $5 million in annual sales their first year, compared to $1.5 to $3 million for a more typical home center. Later Depot stores averaged $40 million or more, but today they are averaging less—slightly more than $30 million, because they have flooded some markets with additional units, taking business away from some of their nearby stores.

Marcus, a charismatic leader, and Blank, a much quieter executive who now owns the Atlanta Falcons pro football team, used to visit all the stores, meet all the employees and establish personal relationships that kept enthusiasm high. Today the company operates nearly 2,000 stores and has some 300,000 employees, making the task more difficult, if not impossible, though its current CEO, Frank Blake, follows the practice to some degree, he says.

What made Home Depot succeed when its copy-cat warehouse competitors did not? Dozens did spring up and then failed. Marcus has a ready and convincing answer:

"It was our culture. We brought together the right combination of 'wild merchants with controls', combined with dedicated employees and tremendous merchandising values. Customers loved the experience of shopping with us."

Marcus' own highly contagious enthusiasm and people-skills also played a major role. He was—and is—a master motivator and communicator. Today he devotes his time to charitable endeavors and bankrolled a marvelous big aquarium in Atlanta.

Another reason Depot succeeded, Marcus recalled, is that they attracted better people by paying more. As mentioned before, most full-time employees became stockholders. He also recalls that the company had always been dedicated to working within each community, supporting local charities, helping out in emergencies, and "being a part of each community." That was different from many of its competitors.

Over the years, the company shifted from a highly promotional format with lots of sales to an Everyday Low Pricing concept, a philosophy espoused by Sam Walton of Walmart and his successor, David Glass. In its early promotional days, Depot executives found it hard to manage inventories as they would sell out of some products, thereby disappointing customers.

While still advertising regularly, Depot's advertising today is not full of huge markdowns and relies more on selling concepts and home improvement ideas, in addition to specific products.

Depot's history deserves more than a casual mention. It not only brought warehouse retailing to the hardware industry around the world, it also introduced warehouse retailing to other channels of trade both here in the U. S. and also overseas. Unfortunately, later it also became a case history of how a management change can damage a company's culture and reputation.

Marcus retired as CEO and was succeeded by Blank, his longtime partner and associate. As Blank neared his own retirement, the General Electric company was in process of selecting its new leader to succeed the legendary Jack Welch. The board picked Jeffrey Immelt, and the top two other candidates decided to seek their future elsewhere. One was a man named Robert (Bob) Nardelli, who had run GE's major appliance division and other business segments very successfully.

Depot hired Nardelli and Blank stepped aside. After 25 years, Home Depot no longer was managed by its founders. At first, Marcus and Blank supported Nardelli's leadership, but that changed as time progressed. In an interview on the company's 25th anniversary when Nardelli had not yet come in for so much criticism, Marcus said, "The company is bigger and more sophisticated than it was under my and Blank's management and it needed a different style of management."

It certainly got that under Nardelli.

One of the first things he did was to centralize operations in Atlanta, bringing into the home office regional and branch operations from around the country. In the process, many longtime Depot executives decided to leave the company rather than relocate to Atlanta. That cost the company a huge load of talent and experience. It also destroyed most of the freedom managers enjoyed in dealing with local opportunities and competition. The entrepreneurial spirit which had bloomed under Marcus and Blank disappeared.

Another quick decision was to convert from many full-time employees to far more part-timers in order to reduce payroll costs. What it really reduced was the company's service. Service suffered tremendously and Nardelli heard about it. The policy was later reversed, but the damage was done. Industry observers still do not believe the service is as good as it once was, even though Frank Blake, who succeeded Nardelli, has been trying to restore the company's culture by enhanced training, once again hiring professionals and using more full-timers. It's easy to lose customers and a reputation; much harder to gain them back.

Nardelli did move the company into technology, relying on his GE experiences. The company upgraded computer systems, even installed self-checkouts, the first in the home center industry, to speed up the checkout process for customers. It also subscribed to UCCnet, which provides item registry and synchronization services that insure standards-compliant data with its suppliers. This aims to reduce errors and supply chain costs.

Another favorable Nardelli decision was to bring in major appliances. Lowe's, another major competitor, had long sold major appliances and was #2 in the nation, lagging only Sears. Today, Depot has become #3 in major appliance sales.

Still another Nardelli decision was to increase margins from the traditional 27% to today's range of about 32+%. Considering that a considerable portion of Depot's sales are in major appliances as well as lower-margined lumber and building material sales, this means that margins on the shelf goods, with which they compete against traditional hardware stores, are higher than they used to be and closer to those of their independent and small-chain competition, except for those items known to be extremely price-sensitive.

Nardelli also created nearly half a dozen specialty divisions, including some wholesaling ones.

As the company's reputation and service deteriorated, the board finally forced Nardelli to leave the company, and under his successor, Frank Blake (also an ex-GE executive), many of Nardelli's actions have been reversed—such as selling off and closing the specialty divisions.

Blake's efforts are still a "work in progress" but he is generally given high marks for the decisions he is making. He calls on stores incognito and checks them out; he began hiring experienced tradesmen again in order to improve service; he brought in more people to man the stores; he has sharply reduced some prices to make the stores more competitive. Employees as well as vendors say he is much more accessible than Nardelli was.

The Lowe's story

As Home Depot began to dominate the home center industry, one of its earliest members began to realize it needed to transform itself.

Lowe's is a postwar success story, much like Walmart, having grown from a Southern small town hardware store into a retailing giant by adapting to changing consumer demands, changing competition and changing opportunities.

From its 1946 start as a hardware store in North Wilkesboro, North Carolina, it first evolved into a lumber-building material retailer catering to the postwar building boom by offering, in addition to hardware products, building materials and then it became a major factor in major appliances.

When it went public in 1961, a typical Lowe's store was located in a small city in the South, averaged 6,000 sq. ft. of showroom space, plus a storage shed for lumber and building material products. Its core customer was a building contractor or tradesman, though hard-core Do It Yourselfers contributed a share of sales.

In that format, local hardware stores did not consider it a major competitor. Most hardware stores did not sell major appliances or building materials. Their ranges of tools, hardware, electrical and plumbing supplies and paint were much broader, their employees more knowledgeable. They managed to live together.

For a couple of years after Depot's opening in 1978 and its remarkable growth, Lowe's did not react, but by 1980, its executives realized they had to further change in order to compete with this exciting new concept. After 1980, it began opening somewhat larger stores and went after consumer (retail) sales much more aggressively. In 1981, for the first, time, Do-It-Yourself sales exceeded those of sales to contractors. This was 3 years after Home Depot came into being.

Its stores, however, continued to be concentrated in the south and mostly in smaller cities, not metro markets.

Its typical stores ranged from 15,000-40,000 sq. ft., plus storage shed, even though it had begun opening "larger" stores in 1989. It had little presence in metro markets where there was more population and higher concentrations of high income DIYers. Lowe's for some years operated with a unique structure. It had 5 key executives guiding it, including a man by the name of Johnny Walker, one of the world's great salesmen, who headed the vital major appliance segment. Another notable member of that group was Robert Strickland, who later became corporate chairman.

Lowe's was surviving. That's more than could be said for the pioneer home centers in metro markets invaded by Home Depot, like St. Louis, Indianapolis, Cleveland, etc.

In 1996, Robert Tillman, a one-time store manager from North Carolina, who had been agitating for even larger stores, was named to succeed one of its longtime executives, Leonard Herring, as president and CEO. He later added the title of chairman, which had been borne by Robert Strickland, another longtime Lowe's leader.

Lowe's today is a testament to Tillman's vision, strategy, and ability to lead and motivate. His vision transformed the company just as dramatically as its founder, Carl Buchan, had when he added building materials and major appliances, and its 1980 move aggressively into consumer sales under the guidance of its then 5-man executive team.

A typical Lowes store front.

Tillman and his team looked at what Depot was doing and decided to improve upon it. Lowe's began moving into metro markets, opened warehouse-type, much larger stores, but made them cleaner, better lit, better signed and more consumer-friendly.

Did it succeed? Yes, and one measure is that Home Depot has now been upgrading its own stores by trying to improve housekeeping, adding better lighting, more signs and generally trying to operate cleaner stores.

Today Lowe's is the #2 home center retailer in the world. It is nowhere near the size of Home Depot, but it is growing at a slightly better rate than Depot.

Lowe's' prototype today is about 121,000 sq. ft., plus a sizeable outdoor garden shop, typically about 30,000 sq. ft. Lowe's stores are actually somewhat larger than the average Depot unit. Lumber is now stored inside. The old outdoor sheds have disappeared in the new format, though some lumber is still stored under cover in the garden center. Its color scheme is light blue, red and grey, contrasted with the famous Home Depot orange.

Lumber is now stored inside Lowe's stores.

By the end of 2001, 50% of its stores were in cities of more than 500,000 population, and today the percentage is greater than 70%. Its stores are averaging less than 5 years in age, contrasted with some of the old (and shopworn) stores of its main rival.

Differences between Lowe's and Depot

When Depot opened, it bypassed the middleman (wholesalers) and had manufacturers ship merchandise directly into each warehouse store. That operational strategy was completely opposite that of Lowe's.

Home Depot bypassed wholesalers and bought direct from manufacturers, with goods shipped to individual stores. The stores were big enough, generating enough volume, to make this possible. Marcus and another home center executive, Frank Denny, who founded Builders Square, felt that the independent manufacturer's representative, used by so many smaller manufacturers, was another unnecessary expense and tried to bypass them. The loss of such sales volume affected many reps, put some out of business but lead to the emergence of a new kind of organization, the "servicing rep", who would go into stores, check stock, write orders and in some cases, clean up and improve store displays.

Lowe's, like Walmart, operates efficient distribution centers to feed its stores with merchandise. Each serves between 50-100 retail units. It is operating nearly a dozen units now. It also operates 13 reload centers, which are used for commodity distribution, mostly bulky building materials. In addition, two specialty distribution centers distribute irregular/non-conveyable merchandise.

While these warehouses require a second handling of merchandise, they also enable individual stores to draw on the DCs in smaller amounts, keeping in-store inventory levels closer to rates of sale. This has another benefit as well, in that merchandise turns at the store level more often and merchandise is not as likely to get dusty or shopworn sitting on shelves too long.

Interestingly, in 2009 Home Depot under its new CEO, Frank Blake, began building its own network of distribution centers, emulating both Lowe's and Walmart. Feeding stores from its own distribution centers should enable Depot to improve stockturns at the store level and have cleaner, fresher merchandise.

Another home center giant emerges

Six years before Marcus and Blank opened the first 3 Home Depots in Atlanta, a man by the name of John Menard opened his own store in a small city in Wisconsin.

While big-city home center pioneers failed competing against Home Depot, Menard has met the challenge. Today his privately owned company is the nation's 3rd largest chain, operating more than 200 stores throughout the Midwest—as far east as Ohio and as far west as Wyoming and as far south as Columbia, Missouri.

Menard stores today offer consumers a shopping difference compared to warehouse formats. Although its stores are huge (some are now 200,000 sq. ft., much larger than either Depot or Lowe's), its stores look more like traditional retail outlets with (high) gondola fixtures, although some warehouse racking can be found more towards the rear of the store.

Menards likes to say it follows the Target mass merchandise concept of wide aisles, well lit stores and tiled floors, not "a grubby warehouse."

Menard stores today are almost sparklingly clean. Floors glisten; housekeeping is excellent. Pricing is very sharp. Two of those 3 descriptive phrases are a far cry from early Menard units, which were unkempt and messy. Lowball pricing, however, has always been a hallmark of this tough competitor.

With its upscale merchandising, the company does a particularly good job in seasonal merchandise such as Trim-A-Tree.

Competitive-pricing research tends to show that Menards is the low price leader, though that fact has been challenged by Home Depot's attorneys.

While once-profitable home center pioneers like Grossman, Ernst Home Centers, Central Hardware and Hechinger caved under the pressure of Home Depot and Lowe's' warehouse formats and cut-throat pricing, Menards found a way to upgrade its stores and attract more women and families by offering them a pleasant shopping environment. It is the only privately-owned home center chain that has been growing at a pace somewhat similar to the two public giants.

Concentrating its growth in the Midwest, Menards is estimated to be doing well in excess of $7 billion in sales, though actual numbers are not known as Menard is famous for not providing any information about its operations.

Industry observers in the U. S. note that any two home center giants appear to be able to survive in any given market, but when a third chain enters a market, competition soon forces the weakest one out. That proved true in the past when a Builders Square or Home Base competed with Home Depot or Lowe's in some markets, but when Lowe's or Depot became a third competitor, the weaker Builders Square or Home Base would lose out.

So far, however, Menards has been surviving in 3-chain markets. Examples are Rockford, Illinois, where Menards was the original big-box retailer and now both Depot and Lowe's also operate there. Indianapolis, Indiana, a much larger market, also has all 3 units there, with Lowe's and Menards being there before Depot also came to town. Builders Square had been there but the 3-chain "rule" made them the weaker and they departed the city before Depot came to town.

Menards is much different than its big publicly owned competitors in many ways, although carrying all the basic hardlines categories, plus lumber and building materials. In 2009 it began adding more cleaning supplies, some clothing and generally trying to appeal more to women and families. It is even selling some food and candy items now.

It is a powerful advertiser, running full color circulars every week in its major markets, all emphasizing price, price, price. Circulars aren't limited to shelf goods; they always feature lumber and building materials as well. It also advertises on TV quite regularly. In some markets, it is the most aggressive advertiser in the home center field, certainly advertising far more regularly than any franchised or dealer-owned hardware group.

The company's own manufacturing facility in Eau Claire, Wisconsin, produces doors, kitchen and bath countertops and picnic tables, boosting profits and helping keep prices down on these big-ticket items.

How is the hardware industry doing now?

It was in the late 60s that the hardware industry began to face its toughest challenges—not just from discounters and larger home centers on a retailing level but from the increasing sophistication of technology and distribution and basic changes in the way Americans lived and worked.

The Universal Product Code came into being; computers began to make their appearance at all levels of hardware distribution—for manufacturers, wholesalers and even retailing; catalog sellers emerged for a time; farm/fleet stores also began to be a competitive factor; downtown shopping areas were declining as outlying shopping centers wooed retailers away from Main Street; a better-educated second or third generation of ownership in some cases decided retailing (or wholesaling or manufacturing) wasn't for them and chose other livelihoods; other kinds of stores began stocking more of the products normally found in hardware stores and lumberyards on a much broader basis—stores like supermarkets, chain drug stores; convenience stores; firms like Family Dollar and Dollar General serving lower-income areas; eventually even the Internet became a competitor, though not just of the hardware industry but every kind of product and form of distribution.

From the 60s on, however, the hardware industry began fighting back. While the number of wholesalers and retailers now in existence is smaller than the number that were operating in the early postwar years, the ones surviving—at both retail and wholesale levels—are far stronger, bigger and more adaptable.

Take wholesaling, for example.   Whereas there once were approximately 550 full line wholesalers, by 2009 the number had declined to less than 100, but those that remain are much larger than ever.   Orgill, based in Memphis, Tennessee, for example, is a privately owned firm now doing more than $1 billion in sales and operating coast to coast as well as internationally.   It grew from a strong regional wholesaler into an international firm.

Other wholesalers grew their own businesses into triple digit sales volumes—firms like The Emery-Waterhouse Co. of Portland, Maine, and House-Hasson Hardware of Knoxville, Tennessee.   There are many others like them.   Surviving dealer-owned wholesalers like Ace, Do it Best Corp.(formerly Hardware Wholesalers, Inc.) and True Value (formerly Cotter & Co.) now are multi-billion dollar distributors and there are also several smaller, successful dealer-owneds operating regionally.

Many smaller wholesalers went out of business because the real estate they owned became more valuable than the returns they were earning as wholesalers. Others closed because younger generations did not want to continue in the business or there were family problems. Still others closed because larger wholesalers simply offered more services or were operating such automated warehouses that old-style distribution centers could not compete from a cost standpoint. Many smaller firms were bought out by other wholesalers. This process was continuing in 2009 as House-Hasson bought Moore-Handley of Alabama after it filed for bankruptcy protection.

Manufacturing underwent similar consolidation as large companies, such as Stanley and Cooper, began buying up family businesses. Allen Petersen, whose family invented the Vise Grip wrench, changed the firm name when he took over to American Tool Co. and also acquired other companies, building the firm into a substantial industry player before selling the company.

From the 1950s on, the National Retail Hardware Association, now known as the North American Retail Hardware Association, and *Hardware Retailing* magazine, operated later for a time as *Do It Yourself Retailing* before changing its name back to *Hardware Retailing*, played important roles.

NRHA launched a series of national consumer promotions focusing on independent retailers. It lined up manufacturers to advertise in national publications and on radio and television. . . provided store decorative kits featuring manufacturers' products to tens of thousands of retail members. . . enlisted wholesalers to support the promotions via their direct mail and other local-level advertising efforts. Thousands of retailers participated in these promotions. It focused the public's attention on independent retailing as it had never been focused before. Consumer contests awarded substantial prizes, and trade contests also rewarded participating retailers. A number of different advertising themes were used, some seasonal, all to the industry's benefit.

Meanwhile, NRHA's magazine dedicated itself to helping retailers (and wholesalers) better meet the challenges of the times. In the mid 1960s, the magazine conducted a 6-month research project among 26 stores scattered across America, tracking consumers and their buying habits.

Research of this type had never before been undertaken in the hardware industry.

It was commonly said by speakers throughout the industry that women comprised about half the customers in a typical hardware store, perhaps because so many stores carried housewares and gift items. The magazine's research proved otherwise. 66% of the customers were men. Average sales per transaction also were charted. Those and other results of the 6-month research project led to NRHA programs to help retailers and wholesalers improve.

Indeed, under Russ Mueller's leadership, NRHA's research department grew considerably and it continued that growth under Bill Mashaw, who took over NRHA when Mueller died. Research services included site evaluations for retailers, market share research for manufacturers—whatever would help the industry became a function of the research department.

NRHA and *Hardware Retailing* conducted marketing seminars around the nation for many years. These free seminars provided manufacturer executives, as well as advertising agency personnel, with information about customer trends, store traffic studies, market size and other industry data that would enable them to better understand—and serve—the hardware industry. Each year, more than 1,000 sales and marketing executives and ad agency people would be updated on current industry trends and events. These informative seminars were free.

Even Mr. Oswald, a cartoon feature the magazine carried for more than 70 years, became involved in the upgrading movement taking place throughout the retail industry. He modernized his store, just as thousands of retailers were doing, and he became a more aggressive advertiser. He spent more time encouraging and training his employees to improve their product knowledge.

The 70s, 80s and onward saw surviving independent hardware retailers, home centers and lumber building material dealers grow their sales, expand their businesses and become a more agile competitor to big-boxes of all kinds, whether mass merchant or home center chain.

They began moving to suburban shopping centers with the advantages of adequate parking and the joint appeal of neighboring strong retailers.

The Mr. Oswald cartoon, portraying the life of a store owner, ran in Hardware Retailing for many decades.

They opened larger stores, and installed new fixtures and brighter décor. They began advertising more and more regularly. State and regional hardware associations developed store planning departments to encourage and help retailers become better merchants. NRHA conducted ongoing training seminars for state and regional association personnel responsible for store planning, to be sure that retailers throughout the country could be assured of the latest and best in store planning. Similar seminars were held for association personnel providing accounting and computer services to members.

More wholesalers began offering store-identity programs, and now dealers were more agreeable to including a group name into their own store name. In pre-war years and in early postwar years, dealers weren't very receptive to that idea. Wholesalers also began promoting these store names, spending a lot of money, much of it solicited from manufacturers, utilizing various kinds of mass media, helping drive traffic to individual stores.

Cotter & Co., with Ed Lanctot spearheading the effort, was the most aggressive, promoting the True Value name. Ace Hardware wasn't far behind. Both chose ex-professional athletes to be spokesmen for their retailers. Ace also used actress Suzanne Somers for a while as a spokesperson.

Millions of wholesaler-produced circulars and catalogs and other mass media advertising spread the names of store groups like Sentry Hardware, Pro Hardware, Ace Hardware, True Value and Do It Best. The independent retailer appeared to have the buying power of a chain store, but still offered his generally renowned better service.

In the late 70s and throughout the 80s, wholesalers also began expanding their store design departments and developed prototype store layouts for their customers, saving them design money as well as assuring a more modern product presentation for consumers. One of the unfortunate by-products of these efforts was the financial impact it had on some state and regional hardware associations, removing one of the major sources of income with which the associations had built staff to provide services to member dealers. In a way, this ultimately helped lead to the demise of some associations since it deprived them of revenue needed to finance personnel to render services to member dealers.

As wholesalers' sales grew, they gobbled up smaller distributors, expanded their territories, built new, more modern distribution centers in order to be more efficient and serve their customers with better service and lower costs. The development of sprawling one-floor, high-ceiling distribution centers was one of the transformational changes wholesaling underwent in the postwar years.

Dealers concentrated on improving employee performance and devoted more time and attention to employee training. The National Retail Hardware Association, now known as the North American Retail Hardware Association, continued providing training materials and increased its efforts. It developed the Advanced Course in Hardware Retailing (ACHR), produced training films for members to use with employees, developed Show-How brochures for consumers that explained how to do home repairs and fix-up projects and made them available at low cost to dealers so they could encourage more Do It Yourself. They would be imprinted with a dealer's name and served as a constant reminder, in the consumer's home, of the helpful hardware man.

Before computers began to appear in retail stores, wholesalers provided a great deal of helpful information to retailers as offshoots of their own computers. Lists of slow-sellers and hot sellers; pricing information; previous market or show purchases. Dozens of different kinds of information like that.

As computers began dropping in price and the concept of computerization became more widespread throughout America, dealers began embracing computerization and stores were tracking merchandise movement, margins, employee productivity. Some wholesalers developed computer systems for their dealers, and then firms like Triad (now Activant), RockSolid and others developed comprehensive computer systems for the industry's retailers. Soon individual retailers began enjoying the same technological kinds of management and merchandising information available to chain store competitors.

The front of a surviving Southern small home center chain.

Second and third generations and entirely new management began taking over retail stores, bringing more modern management to them, including, of course, the ready adoption of computer systems, but also focusing on employee training, better management and accounting, sharper advertising and marketing.

Retailers realized they had to expand their stores, that the small, old-style hardware store or little lumberyard sales area simply wasn't sufficient any more. They needed bigger stores to attract customers as well as to display en masse categories like outdoor living, power lawn care equipment, etc.

In another recognition of reality, hardware retailers and even some lumber/building material retailers began opening on Sundays, a day on which they had been closed in the immediate postwar years, but as mass merchandisers as well as home center chains were open on Sunday, local stores changed. Hours generally are shorter than weekdays, but many retailers report customers waiting for them to open Sunday mornings and sometimes, dealers say, they do more business during Sunday's shorter hours, than they do on a Saturday.

In a number of markets, retailers banded together and began group advertising, sometimes just members belonging to a dealer-owned firm or buying group like Pro or Sentry; other times, retailers in a given market, regardless of buying affiliation, banded together to convince the American consumer that independent stores were able to offer them price, value as well as outstanding service. In many markets, such promotional efforts are continuing.

Whereas in the immediate postwar period many retailers did only a few hundred thousand in sales annually, today many surviving retailers are multi-million retail outlets.

Wholesaler buying markets became more and more important. They introduced hundreds of new, smaller manufacturers and thousands of new items to retailers. They enabled major manufacturers to show more of their product range for retailer evaluation. Retailers could network with fellow retailers and gain sales and promotional insights. Preceding major seasonal opportunities, these markets helped dealers plan for lawn and garden or Christmas selling. Educational seminars were added, helping dealers become better operators, better promoters, more profitable merchants.

Meanwhile, retailers decided that they could offer more and more services in their trading areas, giving consumers more and more reasons to shop at their local hardware store or lumberyard. Services like being a shipping center, renting tools and equipment, selling cell phones or maybe even be a franchised Radio Shack outlet. Whatever the community or area needed and lacked.

Services rendered by retailers vary widely, depending on a store's location, customer needs and employee capabilities.

Retailers searched for and found new and useful items which helped distinguish their inventories from those of the big boxes. One of the ways these searches continue to pay off is by dealers using the Internet to share their experiences and ideas.

John Fix III, a True Value retailer in Eastchester, NY, a New York City suburb, created a blog some years ago called *Hardlines* and several thousand retailers now read messages from each other talking about new products they've discovered that sell well, or question each other to find sources of supply or compare rates of sale on products.

Some wholesalers have created their own blogs so their customers can more easily communicate with buyers and other wholesale personnel. Dealers whose wholesalers don't have such blogs often lobby for them.

Individual retailers set up web sites to sell merchandise off the Internet, and some wholesalers created web sites through which its individual retailers could benefit when consumers bought items off the wholesaler's web site, sometimes delivered to a local dealer for pickup by the consumer at the closest store.

The W. E. Aubuchon Co., mentioned earlier as a pioneer privately owned hardware chain, says its web site is accounting for about $5 million in annual sales, more, in fact, than any of its 120+ stores produce.

It wasn't only mass merchandisers and home centers with which hardware men had to compete. Catalog houses were another threat, especially for housewares and small appliances. That threat finally died off as catalog houses went out of business.

To compete with any and all giant competitors, retailers began developing niche merchandise categories, some as unique as beer and wine-making equipment. Those are just two of the more unusual niches; there are many more less unusual which give retailers a competitive uniqueness in the marketplace. This is an ongoing process. Hardware stores also began stocking some housewares again, after largely giving up the category when they first started to battle home centers and needed to beef up their DIY merchandise. Owners realized that women are the decision-makers in many families and also that many women now live alone and need to be courted just as much as male customers.

Some stores also conduct "women-only" evening seminars and workshops to help customers learn about products and techniques such as antiquing. "Ladies' Night" events are popular promotions staged by many retailers.

In 2008 and 2009, independent hardware stores were helped by the general economy, as consumers and businesses tightened their budgets, cut back on big projects, and began shopping closer to home for smaller fix-it needs. Unfortunately, the economy was not so kind to lumber/building

Retailers recognize the consumer's interest in protecting the environment and are emphasizing such products.

material merchants, especially those more dependent on new home construction or large remodelers.

No one knows the actual store count of surviving independent hardware retailers, home centers and lumber/building material dealers exactly, but research by the Home Improvement Research Institute puts the number of hardware stores at about 20,000+, with several thousand independent home centers and another 15-20,000 lumber yards. For many years, the National Retail Hardware Association estimated that there were upwards of 25,000 retailers. NRHA also estimated that there were 10,000 towns and cities with one or more hardware stores. In 2009, NRHA says there are 20,050 hardware stores, 10,300 lumber/building material dealers and 9,900 home centers. Overall store numbers for the two groups are quite similar. It is clear, however, that modern highway networks as well as competitive pressures have deprived some smaller towns of a "local hardware store or lumberyard."

Why are so many retailers surviving despite so much competition? One reason is the tremendously wide range of products being offered. Surviving retailers are the solution-providers for problems consumers didn't know they had.

They've survived. . . they've modernized. . .they've grown.

Despite everything.

Chapter Four

AN EVER-CHANGING PRODUCT MIX

Over the years, hardware stores have carried a wide range of merchandise in addition to the basics. Lumber/building material merchants, on the other hand, generally concentrated on their basics, adding only some lines that would make them more appealing to Do It Yourselfers and which, ultimately, put them into greater competition with local hardware stores whenever they expanded their assortments.

For example, before and after the war in most of America's small and medium-sized towns and cities, hardware stores stocked a wide range of quality housewares. Housewares of a lesser quality could be found in variety stores, but if you wanted better or top-of-the-line cookware, cutlery, etc. or gifts, your local hardware dealer was the place to go. As small electric appliances made their appearances, they too were to be found in the local hardware store.

Many hardware stores were the gift centers of their community or trading area, especially when wives recognized the importance of appealing to female customers and often were active in the business.

In metro areas where hardware stores were—and are—always considerably smaller and department store competition much greater, retailers stuck very much to the basics since they were serving local tradesmen, apartment owners and local owners as well as renters. Housewares was not a strong category for them, though they generally stocked cleaning supplies to some degree.

For many of the postwar years, food stores sold food; drug stores sold drugs and related items. Specialty gourmet housewares stores were far into the future, in most cities and towns.

Housewares was only one of the categories in which postwar hardware stores dominated.

They were the headquarters for toys, and every Christmas season, toys became a dominant merchandise category, more so, even, than holiday decorations, which for many years were pretty much limited to a few strings of lights for the live Christmas trees sold elsewhere in town. Local variety stores provided some competition for tinsel and other lower cost Christmas decorations.

The big emphasis on Trim-A-Tree and holiday decorations didn't develop for a couple of decades after World War II. The development of long-lasting artificial Christmas trees and the urge to upgrade holiday decorations led retailers into a major new merchandising category, one that came to replace the toy business, which departed to other retailers. This is one category where some retailers do an absolutely outstanding job, in many cases becoming the dominant retailer of the category in their area, while others merely dabble in the category. It is a demanding category, highly specialized and requiring a gambling spirit when buying well ahead of the selling season.

Now, of course, mass merchandisers and other stores, including chain drug stores and home center chains, go after the business, too, but sharp merchants in the hardware trade are still able to compete.

Some hardware stores even carried major appliances, though they were few in number. Others dabbled in furniture, but they were even fewer in number. Occasionally long ago, one could even find the local hardware merchant also a funeral director. Probably none survived in that dual role after World War II.

For the first few decades after World War II, Western Auto and Gamble stores were the primary automotive supply stores in much of the

Midwest, supplemented by Coast to Coast stores. Similar retailers to Western Auto existed in other parts of the country and were the dominant competitors for that category. Virtually all hardware stores carried very basic automotive aftermarket supplies. No hard parts, of course.

Over the years, on a national basis, hardware stores have been in and out of automotive care, sometimes devoting considerable space to the category, then deciding it wasn't generating enough sales to justify that much space and they would cut back. Today all stores continue to carry some basic car-care products, while others see them as a major category. It depends on local competition and management's interest in the category.

Lawn and garden merchandising was in its earliest stages in the immediate postwar period and shortly after. Lawn care was pretty simple. You owned a non-powered, push-type reel mower. You bought some grass seed and maybe a pretty simple fertilizer, though that wasn't at all considered a necessity. Of course, you had to own a rake for leaves and maybe a wheelbarrow. It wasn't until a few years after the war that a man in Minnesota's Twin Cities claimed to be the first to invent a power mower when his firm attached a motor to a reel mower.

Then someone invented another type of power mower, the rotary mower, cheaper to make with a rotating blade, and suddenly, hardware stores began selling mowers costing hundreds of dollars, and the lawn and garden business began to be much more important. Quite suddenly, there were dozens, maybe hundreds of lawn mower manufacturers or assemblers around the country. It was an easy product to manufacture or assemble and market under one's own name.

At first, power mowers were almost a luxury item, their prices were comparatively high, but competition soon took care of that. Prices dropped; the market expanded rapidly.

Local sources eliminated freight costs so locally produced mowers were cheaper. There were, at the start, no strong brand names, so brands didn't matter as much. The hardware man's reputation was enough to convince consumers that the mowers he stocked were good quality and would do the job. Ultimately, of course, many of the early mower makers or assemblers were weeded out as brand names began to be developed, until now the market is dominated by a few giant firms with well established brand names—plus wholesaler-sponsored private brands.

Firms like Scotts and others began developing chemical compounds that would nurture lawns, kill weeds and do other wonderful things for grass and flowers. Average sales increased, and lawn care became something of a status symbol, especially in suburbia.

This burgeoning market also attracted lots of competition as supermarkets, drug stores and discounters decided they should share in this bounty. Lawn and garden specialty chains came and went over the years. As a highly seasonal business, they found it tough to make a profit year-round.

Still, the lawn and garden department has grown into one of the major categories for retailers everywhere, except for densely populated major cities where lawns are virtually non-existent. Hardware and home center retailers continue to win sales because of their superior customer service, their offering of quality products and their extensive assortments. This is especially true of green goods. Major home center chains and Walmart, as the nation's largest mass merchandiser, today maintain large outdoor sales areas of green goods, whereas most hardware stores, lacking that much space, confine their live-goods sales to a few flowers and specialty items. Target, the #2 mass merchandiser, is not much of a competitor in the category because of its location strategy.

Another spring-summer merchandise category that has undergone tremendous change and expansion is outdoor living. From the cheap $9.99 charcoal grill, this merchandise category has exploded into $1,000 gas grills (or higher), a whole array of accessories, outdoor furniture, wading pools, and hundreds of other products. For suburban stores, it, like lawn and garden, is a major sales draw in spring and summer.

Wholesalers have been most helpful in assisting retailers generate sales in these seasonal categories by emphasizing them in circulars and catalogs. Specialty wholesalers also exist in these categories and supply a far broader assortment than traditional wholesalers. When retailers attend wholesaler buying markets, they can review the upcoming seasonal lines, compare features, prices and determine how to position themselves for the coming selling season.

Paint is another basic department that varies in importance based on the kind of competition a retailer faces, together with the amount of space a dealer has and how much he likes the category. All hardware stores carry paint; some do a terrific job with it; others are merely convenience outlets. Most wholesalers today offer a private-brand paint at price-points that keep their retailers competitive in the price game, while retailers often supplement those lower priced products with a major brand name.

A typical store's paint department showing hundreds of paint chips.

Home centers, on the other hand, tend to make the paint department a more important category, in most cases putting the department up front in their stores, many providing sit-down areas where customers (often women) can review paint chips in deciding colors. The large color chip displays now offered by major paint brands demand a lot of space, which makes it difficult for smaller hardware stores to do as well with the category as larger hardware stores and home centers.

Plumbing is an especially interesting category for hardware retailers, home centers and lumber/building material stores. Especially today as price-points for faucets easily are in the triple-digit range. Smaller stores focus on the basics and offer little selection, whereas larger stores and home centers emphasize style and design and enjoy upgraded sales because they appeal to the stylish tastes of their customers, again appealing to women. Home centers are devoting plenty of space to model bathrooms and kitchens to encourage the sale of plumbing items and the other merchandise needed in these expansions and remodelings.

Electrical products have undergone a great many packaging improvements in these days of self-service. Planograms now make the presentation of these products more impressive in retail stores as well as easier for consumers to shop. Assortments have grown too, of course.

One category that varies widely in its importance to retailers is sporting goods. In some stores and in some regions of the country, hardware retailers are the dominant outlet for these products. It depends, in many cases, on the interests of management. Almost every store carries a smattering of sporting goods, but in some stores, it becomes the biggest or next to the most important category. Hunting and fishing supplies dominate in cases like that. Years ago, Winchester-Western, a major vendor, produced a how-to manual for retailers called "Hunting for Profit" that outlined a wide range of modern merchandising and management techniques to help hardware and sporting goods retailers improve their performance.

Tools have been both a basic department as well as a problem for hardware retailers and, to a lesser extent, for lumber/building material retailers. Mass merchandisers and chain home centers have been concentrating their attention on power tools to the degree that some hardware retailers have either eliminated power tools entirely or severely restricted their assortment. Hand tools haven't suffered the same assortment attrition. Hand tool manufacturers seem to be working more closely with wholesalers and retailers. One manufacturer, family-owned Channellock, Inc., in 2009 established a special product relationship with Do it Best Corp., the nation's second largest hardware wholesale firm.

By staging twice-a-year buying markets, wholesalers continue to expose a lot of new products to retailers. Manufacturers know that they need to supplement their longtime standard items at these shows with new, different or improved products to keep retailer interest high. They've also developed plan-o-grams and end cap displays to help retailers introduce new categories and maximize sales from these new products. Over the years, manufacturers have continued to make packaging improvements which encourage consumers to tackle projects once performed only by tradesmen. Packaging improvement with how-to instructions is a never-ending process.

A speaker at a conference once described the wife as "the president of the home", a rather apt description of the style decision-maker for many products carried by hardware, home center and lumber/building material dealers. Smart retailers know this and try to satisfy those presidents.

Over the years, the National Retail Hardware Association's trade publication, *Hardware Retailing* (later renamed *Do It Yourself Retailing*) tried to help retailers establish themselves as leaders in emerging categories by featuring a series of articles called "Profit Opportunities", which outlined research as to market potential, competitive retailers and even produced suggested basic inventories and pricing information.

Those sections recounted the success of retailers already active in those merchandise categories to encourage more retailers to determine if there were opportunities for them as well in their marketing area.

One of the most fascinating things over the years about the hardware industry, especially the retail side of the business, is how entrepreneurial retailers are and how they identify and develop merchandising categories that are unique. For example, retailers in the past and currently are selling such things as clothing, metal detectors, water gardening supplies, wood pellet stoves. It is almost an endless list.

We also remember a lumber/building material down in Texas who sold fabric and sewing supplies and did a thriving business in that niche department, which was housed in a quite fancy showroom along with a splendid display of high end cabinet hardware, door hardware, and bathroom fittings, etc., which would appeal to the women checking out his fabrics.

Luckily, we never heard of any husbands shooting him when their wives succumbed to his high-end presentations.

Chapter Five

THE MANUFACTURER IN POSTWAR TIMES

In pre-war times and in the early postwar years, manufacturers serving the hardware industry were largely family-owned businesses, like the retailers and wholesalers who were their customers. Some were surprisingly large, but most were smaller and a great many were quite small.

Some served only a small trade area, often dictated by the costs of transporting their products, which limited them to serving local wholesalers and retailers. Others, some of them family-owned, however, had grown into national sources of supply.

The oldest manufacturer serving the industry still in business is the forerunner of today's Ames True Temper. The O. Ames Co. actually began in 1774 when John Ames began making shovels. Through wars, depressions and booms (and a variety of owners), it has continued operating, acquiring other companies along the way and developing a wider range of products.

After World War II, materials such as steel, copper and many others were removed from allocation and released for consumer products. During the war, all of these materials had been used in fighting the war. The wartime allocations caused a pent-up demand for many products, which, in turn, gave the industry unprecedented sales growth following the war.

When all those returning service men and women came back home and began forming families, housing demand zoomed and so did demand for the products found in hardware stores and lumber/building material outlets.

There were only a few publicly-owned manufacturing companies in the immediate postwar period, but as time progressed, that began changing, and for many of the same reasons change was occurring in the wholesaling and retailing sides of the industry.

Second or third generations sometimes didn't have the skills or desire to keep a business going and growing, or maybe they didn't enjoy the business and chose to become professionals in other fields, like medicine or law. And sometimes, of course, competition became so fierce that they simply decided to sell out, either to another family-owned business or to a larger firm. Early on, the biggest public company was The Stanley Works, which produced a wide range of tools and a diversified portfolio of hardware products.

Another was the Black & Decker Co., which almost single-handedly created the consumer power tool industry in the postwar years. Management recognized the demand for power tools that was going to be created in the postwar housing boom. It found a way to reduce the cost of producing its standard 1/4" drill and electrified the world with a $9.99 power drill. Other modestly priced power tools were soon developed. Skil Corp., maker of the best selling powered circular saw, also found ways to reduce the cost of its tools and joined in creating the modern power tool industry. It is now owned by Bosch, a multi-national company.

Other companies entered the field—Rockwell Tools, Portable Electric Tools, etc.—but one by one, they dropped out of the picture. Today Black & Decker remains a prominent player in the field as does Bosch. Private brands also are more important today, with both Home Depot and Lowe's emphasizing them. In a much earlier time, the only major private brand was Sears' Craftsman in both hand and power tools.

Cooper, another large public company, began aggressively buying private businesses and soon compiled a broad portfolio of well known brands, such as Lufkin tapes, Wiss shears and garden tools, Nicholson files, Plumb striking tools and Campbell Chain products. Stanley was another buyer, but it did so a bit more quietly than Cooper and did not keep most of the acquired brand names, converting most to the better known Stanley label. Later, the Newell company, under its second-generation leader, Dan Ferguson, began acquiring companies, not only in the hardware field but in housewares as well, gobbling up privately owned companies as well as smaller publicly-owned companies.

Its biggest acquisition was the Rubbermaid Co., and that resulted in the firm's name being officially changed to Newell Rubbermaid, in order to capitalize on the strong brand recognition of the Rubbermaid name. The company even has expanded into the office products field. Newell had little consumer recognition, certainly negligible compared to that of Rubbermaid, although some of its acquisitions did have strong brand recognition. When it bought American Tool Co., it added Vise Grip and other lines American Tool had acquired and then began marketing them all under the Irwin label.

More recently, Scotts Miracle Gro, once known as O. M. Scott Co., the lawn care firm, is the latest major company becoming an aggressive acquisitor, having acquired several companies in order to broaden its line and become a more important vendor to all its customers. Its biggest was Miracle Gro, which it added to its own name, becoming Scotts Miracle Gro.

As this book was being readied for publishing in November 2009, two of the industry's biggest and best known manufacturers, Stanley and Black & Decker, announced that they planned to merge to form an $8 billion manufacturing giant, with Stanley's CEO running both companies and the merged company to be known as Stanley Black & Decker. There is little overlap in the product lineups of the two companies, but the proposed merger still had to be approved by government regulators before being finalized.

Relationships between manufacturer and wholesaler were based on friendship as well as product in the early postwar years, and that has continued until the present, though today, relationships are a good deal more business-based. The buying power of giant retailers puts more pressure on manufacturers today than was the practice for many years after World War II.

Over the years, wholesalers and manufacturers met informally as well as formally at joint meetings conducted by their respective trade associations. Atlantic City, New Jersey, in its heyday, was for many years the gathering place of the joint sessions for the American Hardware Manufacturers Association and the National Wholesale Hardware Association. Similar meetings were held with members of the Southern Wholesale Hardware Association and on a smaller scale with members of the Texas Wholesale Hardware Association. Even smaller meetings between top wholesale and manufacturing executives took place in plush places like Colorado's Broadmoor and California's Pebble Beach.

Here old relationships were strengthened and new ones established. Problems could be discussed and solutions sought.

But increasing pressures were being felt throughout the industry. The emergence of giant retailers in non-traditional retail fields, which began carrying products stocked by traditional hardware and lumber/building material retailers, meant that manufacturers had to decide on a sales policy. Would they sell to these outlets, and if so, how would those sales affect their traditional distribution?

If they decided not to sell to them and lesser brands did, would that cut into their own sales and advance the stature, sales and market share of the secondary brands?

This growing power of larger retailers included mass merchandisers and discounters, beginning with E J Korvette, Masters, and then ultimately to giants like Target, Kmart and, of course, Walmart. Pressure was also being brought to bear on manufacturers by home center chains, first from the pioneer chains, mentioned elsewhere in this book, and then tremendous pressures by Home Depot, whose entire strategy was based on buying direct and bypassing distributors. Lowe's, of course, had always been buying directly from manufacturers and feeding its stores through its own distribution centers.

Manufacturers reacted in different ways. Some resisted for a considerable time, then ultimately recognized reality. Others immediately sold to these newer customers. Traditional wholesalers and retailers also learned to accept reality, though they never liked it. In many categories, shifts in market share became so apparent that they forced the hand of manufacturers who might have been slow to recognize the changes taking place in product distribution.

Some wholesalers developed who specialized in feeding the discount chains as they spanned the country. The services these "feeders" offered, besides the merchandise itself, included stock-checking, housecleaning, order-writing as well as advice on regional product selections and assortments.

Other changes were taking place. Packaging was becoming much more important in virtually every merchandise category. It wasn't enough to simply make a good product. You had to package it smartly, apply a UPC code, provide use instructions, develop merchandise presentations and offer display suggestions to customers. And increasingly, you had to support it with advertising.

You had to improve your catalog pages, adopt microfiche when it became widely used and still later, bring the Internet into your marketing strategy. As the years went by, manufacturers began taking on more of the in-store marketing and merchandising of their products in order to stimulate retail sales. They developed plan-o-grams to help retailers make the most efficient and forceful use of display space. . . they created end cap displays to feature seasonal and new items. . . in more recent times they have been developing clip-strip promotions which are especially effective selling concepts for lower priced and smaller items which can be merchandised in multiple locations in retail stores.

While co-op advertising funds might have been offered previously, the demand for them grew over the years, especially as wholesalers developed direct mail circulars for retailers and as giant chains demanded local advertising assistance.

For many years, many manufacturers did little or no advertising; others relied mainly on their ads in the industry's numerous trade publications. As the retail market continued to diversify with products appearing in more and more retail channels, additional trade magazines came into being or existing ones in these new trade channels had to be considered in one's marketing plans. A great many manufacturers serving the hardware industry spent most of their advertising dollars in the trade press, not the consumer press. Those manufacturers were committed to developing brand aware-ness among retailers and wholesalers, figuring this would ultimately give them exposure at store level to the ultimate consumer. As time went on, however, consumer advertising became more and more important for many products that had never communicated to the consumer before.

The National Retail Hardware Association played a major role in try-ing to keep the consumer's attention focused on "traditional" channels of retailing by developing industry-wide promotions paid for by manufactur-ers, coordinated by NRHA and involving manufacturers, wholesalers and retailers alike.

These efforts were later succeeded by wholesalers' own promotions as store-identity programs became more widespread. Manufacturers were asked to underwrite sponsorship of radio, TV and magazine advertising for Ace stores, for True Value stores, for Trustworthy or Pro stores, and, as some manufacturers said, "and ad infinitum".

Technological changes in products, in production processes as well as in marketing and distribution continue to demand highly skilled partici-pants in the manufacturing sector. Unless manufacturers were committed to "keeping up with the times" and later to cope with the flood of lower priced imports coming into America from overseas, manufacturing became a tough business, just as wholesaling and retailing were, due to postwar changes and challenges. In the search for lower prices, manufacturers often followed low labor costs around the world.

And yet, many of the nation's—and in some cases, the world's—well known brand names are family names—names like Estwing hammers and related tools. . . .Vaughan & Bushnell for striking tools. . . Ali abrasive products. . . . Johnson levels . . . Hudson sprayers and dusters. . . and many, many others—too many to list in their entirety.

Other major brands produced by family-owned firms today include Hyde Tools, Channellock, Chamberlain garage door openers, Fluidmaster, Lasko Products, Lavelle Industries, M. K. Morse, Marshalltown, Toggler, Mr. Longarm, Oatey, Protective Coatings, Seymour of Sycamore, and dozens, if not hundreds, of others.

While many family-owned firms remain a powerful force in the industry, many of the smaller regional firms have disappeared over the years, due to competitive pressures or sometimes an unwillingness to invest far more capital to upgrade facilities, systems, marketing or distribution. As mentioned before, some sold out to larger firms. Such a comprehensive list would be a disturbing reminder of just how competitive the hardware/home center industry has become in the postwar years.

Marketing during the immediate postwar period was much simpler than today. Fair Trade, when it existed, played a role during that era because it assured certain margins for wholesalers and retailers, lost when discounting began and Fair Trade gradually disappeared. Immediately after the war, some manufacturers placed their products on allocation and in some cases even created some of this pent-up demand. Pricing to the trade was based on the "selling price day of shipment." That kind of "marketing" would not be acceptable today.

The manufacturer's representative

One of the interesting facets of the manufacturing sector is the role that independent manufacturers' representatives have played in the industry. So many manufacturing firms have been (and some still are) so small and the United States so large that companies could not afford their own sales forces to cover all 48 (now 50) states.

Only a few large manufacturers operated with their own sales force; the vast majority came to rely on men (and gradually, women) who lived, worked in and covered different areas of the country and represented not just their company but other, non-competitive companies that would be of interest to the wholesalers and retailers in that section of the country. These "reps", as they soon came to be known, might represent half a dozen to a dozen different companies, and would work with maybe 2 to half a dozen different buyers at a wholesale firm or a retail chain.

Representing multiple companies, they could afford to make regular personal calls on prospects within their sales areas—even to smaller firms.

They established valuable personal relationships with buyers that a factory's own sales force could not, in part because they were not visiting buyers as frequently and in part because they simply could not be as aware of local marketing and competitive conditions as would a rep who lived in and worked that territory on a daily basis.

Manufacturers' reps representing multiple companies could thus afford to travel to smaller or somewhat "distant" customers and prospects within their given trade territory, because they had an opportunity to make sales to several buyers. They also developed close relationships with buyers, a thorough understanding of the ways in which each customer did business. They could work buying markets, which wholesalers increasingly began conducting once or twice a year. Manufacturers using reps knew their sales costs in advance—a flat % of sales paid to reps as a commission. In most cases, the commissions paid to them by their manufacturing sources were far less than the cost of a factory's own sales force, with the added advantage of their being local, well known and able to provide better service than a far-off factory could.

The size of the manufacturer using a rep sales force was not always a factor in the decision to use reps. General Electric, Honeywell, even Stanley, used reps in some special situations, special markets or market segments.

But times changed for reps, just as they have been changing for factories, wholesalers and retailers.

The advent of high volume retailers meant that some of these customers did not want to deal with manufacturers' agents or reps. In some cases, strictly from an ego standpoint, they wanted to deal with someone "from the home office." In other cases, they wanted a decision-maker on hand who could give them a "yes" or "no" answer when they hit the factory up for special deals, discounts or what-have-you.

One thing factory personnel noted about some of the retail outlets these chains were opening—the use of so many part-time employees at the store level meant that displays were not kept up as they should be and consequently, the factory's products might not be selling at the rate they should.

This led to the emergence of a new kind of factory rep—the servicing rep. These are people—most frequently women—who will, almost always at the factory's expense, go into a chain's stores, check stock, re-arrange and clean up displays and write orders for merchandise that is needed. In many cases, traditional rep agencies established divisions to do this work. In other cases, completely new servicing agencies came into being.

Today the evolution of the manufacturing sector continues.

While private brands existed for decades even before World War II, the use of such brands, built around the wholesaler's name or the retail chain's name, is greater today than ever before, simply because there are multi-billion dollar wholesalers or wholesale buying groups and many billion-dollar retail chains. and they possess the means, desire and wherewithal to promote the brands.   Sears' Craftsman, Diehard and Weatherbeater are some of the industry's best known private brands—in the minds of most American consumers today, national brands.

It used to be that only "secondary" manufacturers, lacking a strong brand name of their own, would produce private brands, but that distinction disappeared years ago. Today many major brands are willing to make store brands for their best customers.

There has been a great deal of consolidation in the manufacturing sector. Factories bought out weaker competitors. . . .began buying products from overseas. . . in some cases closing out their domestic operations and moving all production to China or other offshore, lower-cost facilities. Most of these actions were the result of the competitive pricing pressures of their customers and, to a lesser degree, to try to keep foreign manufacturers out of the U. S. distribution system. Another evolutionary factor is distributors and major retail chains sourcing directly from overseas, another pressure on U. S. manufacturers.

The process is ongoing, and always will be.

Chapter Six

SOURCES OF SUPPLY

No retailer of any kind wants to rely on a single source of supply. That just isn't in a retailer's DNA. Hardware retailers and lumber/building material dealers may be less inclined that way than any other kind of retailer, in part because of their inherent independence but also because so many of them develop specialty departments or tailor their assortments to unique opportunities in their trading area.

This reluctance to rely entirely on a single source is one reason that pure franchises have had such a difficult time over the years.

The men and women operating Coast to Coast stores, Gamble stores, Western Auto, etc., sometimes found that other wholesalers could supply them with some of the same items as their franchiser could—and at a lower cost. Those were too tempting to pass up.

While thousands of retailers today are concentrating more of their purchases with their primary wholesaler source than ever before (i.e., Ace, Orgill, True Value, Do it Best or a Pro or Sentry distributor), few if any of those dealers give their primary source 100% of their business.

Retailers in this industry, regardless of size, have always had a choice of sources. At one time, there were more than 550 wholesalers that carried broad assortments of most of the basic departments a retailer stocked. For many years both before and after World War II, a retailer's primary source would be several of these so-called full-line wholesalers—not mainly just one. These several distributors carried products from most, if not all, of the basic departments—hardware, tools, paint and paint sundries, plumbing and electrical items. They oftentimes offered different brands within product categories, so retailers could select the brands most preferred in their marketing area. Many wholesalers also carried some of the other products, such as housewares, sporting goods, toys, automotive car-care items. Others largely restricted themselves to the basic categories.

In the early postwar years, before transportation improvements and the interstate highway system transformed America, a great many full-line wholesalers operated within a relatively narrow geographic radius, but as both trucks and highways improved and as some wholesalers gained scale, larger firms began to offer much more competition to smaller local distributors, eventually putting most of them out of business.

Within the last 25 years, the number of full line wholesalers has been steadily declining for a variety of reasons. Today it is estimated to be less than 100. Some say even less.

While full-line wholesalers are the most important sources for most kinds of retailers in the marketplace, dealers also have always turned to specialty distributors, which carry larger inventories in certain specific categories, frequently know the merchandise better, and can provide the items a retailer needs to differentiate himself and his store from competition.

Full-line wholesalers typically stocked from 20-30,000 stockkeeping units; a few as many as 40,000 and some today say they are stocking 60,000 or so. That might mean 2,000 or so stockkeeping units in sporting goods, for example, spread over team sports, hunting, fishing and other sports activities, whereas a specialty distributor in the sporting goods field might carry 5,000 or more items of fishing tackle, guns and ammunition and team sports.

The same is true of other specialized merchandise categories.

And, of course, there are some manufacturers whose whole strategy is built on selling direct to retailers, which includes many of the major paint manufacturers, some power equipment firms and others. Yes, retailers had—and have—plenty of sources of supply.

Retailers often distinguish themselves from competition by dominating categories, such as this cookie cutter display.

The emergence and increasing importance of niche categories at retail is making the role of the specialty distributor even more important to many retailers. How many full-line wholesalers, for example, are carrying beer and wine-making supplies, which some hardware stores are now developing as distinguishing niches for themselves? Or how many are stocking artificial flowers, which are being sold in the housewares departments of many stores today? Or carry metal-finding tools for beach-combers and other scavenging consumers?

Every year, hundreds of new manufacturers enter the hardware indus-try. Many introduce their products at the National Hardware Show®, which spotlights new products from new producers as well as from estab-lished manufacturers in its NEW PRODUCTS EXPOSITION. Here retailers and wholesalers can concentrate their search for "something new" and then go to the vendor's stand to explore pricing and sales discussions.

Similarly, each wholesaler's buying market always includes new products being introduced as new additions to the wholesaler's merchandise offering. Some wholesalers are now following the Hardware Show model by spotlighting new products in a special display, making it easier for buyers to find and evaluate them.

Wholesalers, like retailers, understand it is important to spice up one's standard assortment with interesting new products.

The Internet is now making it possible for retailers across the country to share ideas on hot-selling new items as well as where to buy them or where to buy hard-to-find items. *Hardlines*, the blog developed by John Fix III, a True Value dealer from New York state, is a classic case-in-point. Retailers share success stories about new items they are selling and regularly query each other as to sources of supply for them or simply alternate sources for unusual items in their regular inventories.

In today's competitive retailing field, one of the ways in which independent retailers are succeeding is by distinguishing their offerings from chain stores by searching out useful, interesting new items to satisfy needs American consumers may not have realized they have—until they found the items in their local store.

Chapter Seven

WHOLESALING'S CHANGING ROLE

When World War II ended, there were about 550 full-line hardware wholesalers serving the industry. Many were quite small; only a few were considered "large", though large at the time would be considered small by 2009.

Some states had a surprising number of wholesalers, considering their size and population. West Virginia, for example, had several dozen. Because of that state's geography, many wholesalers served a very small region—a valley or two, where their products could be economically transported to hardware stores, lumberyards and general merchandise stores in that region.

Texas, not surprisingly, also had a lot of wholesalers, but its reason was its huge size. At one time, the Texas Wholesale Hardware Association consisted of 44 member firms. Today there are 6 wholesalers still headquartered in the state. Of course, other wholesalers supply Texas stores, too.

As America was emerging as a country a hundred or more years ago, certain areas became distribution centers as the country moved westward. Minneapolis and St. Paul, as well as Duluth, Minnesota, for example, were headquarters for moving merchandise into the Dakotas and even Montana, though Montana in the postwar days did have one or two of its own hardware wholesalers. Chicago was another major distribution hub, as was

St. Louis, Missouri.   Memphis and New Orleans were strong distribution centers in the South.

Most wholesalers were privately owned, just a few were cooperatives, owned by the retailers who bought from them.   Many of the privately owned wholesalers originated as retailers, who grew and were so successful that they began supplying other retailers and eventually concentrated on the wholesaling side of their businesses.

One such firm, founded in 1842, is still in business, having expanded from a small territory into a number of other states and having acquired a number of its competitors over the years.   That pioneer wholesaler, which believes it is the oldest surviving wholesaler in the industry, is The Emery-Waterhouse Co. of Portland, Maine.   Not only is it the oldest wholesaler in the United States, it is the oldest surviving business of any kind in its home city of Portland.

Emery-Waterhouse's story is similar to that of many other wholesalers, although some of the others which acquired neighboring firms did not survive as it has survived.   It began acquiring other firms over the post-war years, and as it did so, it expanded beyond its New England base into the Mid Atlantic States and upstate New York, even into parts of Michigan. Originally, it served only a part of its home state of Maine.

Another pioneer wholesaler is Orgill, founded in Memphis in 1847. Like Emery, it bought out other firms over the years, but has greatly expanded on its own.   Privately owned by Joe Orgill, it has grown to be the largest non-dealer-owned wholesaler in the United States.   It was run for many years by Bill Fondren, who later moved up to chairman of the corporation.   Ron Beal currently serves as president.   From its original single warehouse location in Memphis, the company has expanded into multiple warehouses around the country in order to serve retailers everywhere.   It now is operating in a number of international countries, as well.

Today, it is estimated that there are less than 100 full-line hardware wholesalers serving the nation's tens of thousands of independent and small chain hardware stores, home centers and lumberyard/building material retailers.   Some industry observers think the number is substantially less.

Three kinds of wholesalers

In the postwar period, there were 3 kinds of full-line wholesalers, although two dominated—the privately-owned or publicly-owned firms and the dealer-owned cooperatives. The third kind, a smaller number, flourished for a relatively brief period and then almost completely disappeared—the cash-and-carry wholesaler.

That wholesaling is a rough business is best documented by pointing out that some dealer-owned cooperatives, which claimed to be the best choice for independents, also did not survive the turbulent times. They were bought out or simply disappeared, as happened to some of the privately- owned firms. Among the casualties were Franklin Hardware Supply of Philadelphia, Walter H. Allen Co. of Texas, Northern Hardware out of Oregon, and Great Western Hardware out of the Los Angeles area.

Larger dealer-owneds also were acquired, the two most notable being Our Own Hardware out of Minneapolis, bought by Hardware Wholesalers, Inc., of Ft. Wayne, Indiana (now Do it Best) and ServiStar, which originally was named American Hardware Supply Co. and began in Pittsburgh as one of the pioneer firms in the dealer-owned segment of the industry. Our Own Hardware was the other pioneer dealer-owned firm. ServiStar was merged with Cotter & Co. and became part of what is now known as True Value.

Today, three of the dealer-owned companies are multi-billion dollar firms, and there are several other smaller firms serving smaller regions. The 3 largest operate nationwide as well as internationally. Indeed, Ace, True Value and Do It Best customers can be found in as many as 60 or more countries around the world.

The other regional dealer-owned firms are United Hardware Supply out of Minnesota, established shortly after World War II, Handy Wholesale Hardware Co. of Texas, which was organized in 1954 and Standard Hardware Distributing, serving New England out of New Hampshire.

Among the other full-line firms, the largest, most aggressive and most successful is Orgill, now operating nationally and doing more than $1 billion in annual sales. One of the first wholesalers to operate a modern one-story distribution center, it now operates multiple DCs around the country. It too is a multi-national retailer, serving customers around the world.

Even the 3 largest dealer-owned firms began as regional wholesalers, with Ace beginning in Chicago and gradually expanding into states adjacent to Illinois. Do it Best, founded as Hardware Wholesalers, Inc., is based in Ft. Wayne, Indiana, and it too was originally a Midwest distributor. It was different from Ace and True Value because it started out serving lumber/building material dealers as well as hardware stores and included lumber and building materials in the merchandise offered to retailers.

In fact, by serving lumber/building material dealers and providing them with hardware products and making some building material products available to hardware stores, this was an early-stage version of a home center.

The newest of the "big 3" wholesalers is True Value, founded by John Cotter as Cotter & Co. in 1948. Ace Hardware is the oldest of the three firms, although it did not begin as a dealer-owned firm. It was founded by 5 Chicago-area retailers, the dominant one being Richard (Dick) Hesse, who took over management of the wholesale firm as it began to grow. Upon his death, the company became a dealer-owned firm.

The third and smallest type of wholesaler was (and is) cash-and-carry. These firms, which thrived in densely populated sections of the east and Midwest in the 60s, 70s and 80s, served predominantly small neighborhood independently-owned hardware dealers plus some lumber yards and later, some independently owned home centers.

A cash-and-carry wholesaler typically carried about 15,000 SKUs, less than a full line wholesaler. It concentrated on the best selling items. The best-selling departments generally were plumbing and electrical, hardware and paint sundries.

The vast majority of cash-and-carry customers would come from within a 50-mile radius, which might mean about an hour's drive to a distribution center to obtain new merchandise. A few would drive even greater distances, but they were a minority.

Its customers were neighborhood, local hardware stores, often affiliated with a co-op or belonging to a stores program, but who were in need of quick replenishment on a regular basis. A good cash-and-carry became a strong second source. A very few retailers visited the cash-and-carry firms on a daily basis, more just once a week and even more made such

Typical high-cube modern Do it Best distribution center supplying retailers.

buying visits on a monthly basis. Average transaction sizes varied widely, depending on how frequently a retailer shopped at the cash-and-carry as well as the season of the year and the retailer's own sales volume.

The cash-and-carry concept continues to be a most effective source of supply for retailers in England, where distances are shorter and retailers there are much smaller in physical size and retail volume than surviving retailers in the U. S. It makes sense for them to buy in smaller quantities from a cash-and-carry firm since their stores are too small to stock deep inventories.

Cash-and-carry wholesalers began to have problems when home centers focused their expansion plans on major metro markets, particularly along the East Coast. They became so dominant in these markets that they forced many smaller hardware stores out of business or store owners decided to retire, and cash-and-carries lost much of their customer base.

They emerged in the U. S. in the early to mid 1960s. Nuway Distributors, reportedly the largest, opened in 1964 in the Baltimore/Washington, DC, area. At its peak, it did close to $50 million in sales. Like some conventional wholesalers, two of its founders had owned and operated a retail store prior to opening Nuway, and another had worked for a traditional wholesaler.

As near as can be determined, there may be 3 remaining firms— Blackwood Supply out of Pittsburgh; Right-Way Dealer Warehouse in Brewster, New York area and B. E. Atlas out of Chicago. Blackwood today is not really a "full-line" distributor, since it only carries 9,000 SKUs from 235 manufacturers but it is operating on a cash-and-carry basis.

Cash-and-carry firms served a very valuable function, offering small retailers an opportunity to frequently and immediately replenish stock in small quantities and at favorable pricing. Typically, they operated at distributor cost plus 10%, although they kept rebates and other negotiated discounts so their actual gross margins were closer to 20%.

However, surviving retailers buying from them kept growing in size and began to give more of their purchases to conventional wholesalers like Orgill or others serving their trade territory or joined one of the 3 major dealer-owned firms, where they could get competitive pricing as well as other services, such as computer-generated bin tickets and price stickers.

Merchandising Groups

One way in which wholesalers have survived is by joining buying/merchandising wholesaling groups. Originally conceived by privately owned wholesalers as a means of fighting corporate chains and later, dealer-owned wholesalers, today some of the groups include smaller dealer-owned firms as members.

The oldest such group was Liberty Distributors, founded during the Depression and led for many years by William George Steltz, Sr., president of Supplee-Biddle-Steltz Co., a Philadelphia distributor. The group's headquarters was in Philadelphia, in a building across the street from Supplee's headquarters. It had its own buying staff, but was heavily influenced by its proximity to its founder's facilities and staff and his dominant personality.

Steltz served as managing director, overseeing the Liberty office and its buyers, until his death in late1958. In 1959, the group appointed its first full-time managing director, Bob Vereen, who had been managing editor of *Hardware Retailing* magazine. Vereen served as managing director for a little over 3 years, then returned to the National Retail Hardware Association as editor of the magazine.

As an independent CEO, he spent his time traveling to member wholesalers and working with the buyers of member companies in order to leverage the group's potential buying power, something that had never previously been achieved. He also recruited additional member wholesalers.

He increased the number and quality of direct mail advertising offered to retailers through Liberty members and upgraded the quality of private brand merchandise as well as the packaging and promotion of those lines.

He tripled the business in 3 years and after he departed, the group chose an executive from Western Auto, the large automotive retail company, who took over and expanded the organization. One major decision was to move the company to the Chicago area, closer to most of its members and to separate it from being in the shadow of Supplee-Biddle-Steltz. Under Vereen's successor, Erwin Croissant, and Croissant's successor, Bill Hooten, Liberty continued to grow, offer new services and become a more essential part of members' survival strategy.

Meanwhile, another ex-wholesale executive, who had been with Janney, Semple, Hill & Co.. out of Minneapolis, formed another merchandising group, Pro Hardware. Paul Cosgrave was his name. Cosgrave envisioned Pro as both a buying group as well as a store identity program for retailers. It developed private brands, model store layouts, store identification programs and, of course, consumer advertising. Another ex-Janney man, Harold Dungan, ran the organization for many years after Cosgrave stepped aside. Paul's son, Gary, continues the Cosgrave involvement in the privately-owned organization as chairman. The organization continues to this day, with Pro stores to be found in many parts of the country.

Pro has diversified and now has divisions serving independent specialty retailers and wholesalers. Each Pro wholesaler today recognizes one of its Pro retailers as the Pro Retailer of the year for that distributor and the winner is further recognized as the Paul Cosgrave Retailer of the Year nationwide.

Other groups also formed, chief among them Sentry Distributors, based in Cleveland, and "fathered" by Norm Luekens, president of The George Worthington Co. of that city. It later merged with Liberty and became Distribution America as the consolidation among wholesalers reduced the membership rolls of both Sentry and Liberty.

Several other smaller merchandising groups also were formed and are still in existence—Val-Test Group and Reliable Hardware Distributors. These generally serve smaller regional and/or specialty wholesalers. Their web sites explain their services, membership characteristics and provide other valuable information about the two organizations.

What the groups offered members were economies of scale in purchasing as well as in producing direct mail advertising for retail customers. Millions of circulars or catalogs, instead of several hundred thousand, meant lower prices for dealers. Combined buying power also meant lower prices for merchandise featured in direct mail advertising, helping retailers be more competitive in an ever more competitive marketplace.

Some of the wholesaler groups, Liberty Distributors in particular, were very active in developing private branded products. Under Vereen, Liberty began coordinating packaging colors from one vendor to another, which had not previously been accomplished, improved the marketing messages and information provided in packaging and literature and, most important of all, developed a one-year-over-the-counter replacement guarantee for a line of Dainty Maid electric appliances, which boomed the business and gave retailers stocking Dainty Maid appliances a powerful marketing tool against the catalog showrooms which were footballing national brand pricing at the time.

These changes made Liberty brands become a more important selling tool for retailers stocking the products.

Trustworthy, a Liberty brand name for male-oriented merchandise, is now used by some wholesalers as a store identity name for their retailers.

Specialty distributors

Retailers also bought—and continue to buy— merchandise from many other, generally smaller distributors—specialty firms generally operating in a single merchandise category, such as sporting goods or housewares.

There were and continue to be thousands of these firms, most of them relatively small, but there are some large ones. In fields like lawn and garden power equipment, where product knowledge is especially important and where retailers need to rely on qualified help, they prove especially helpful.

Wholesale associations served members

For many years, most full line wholesalers belonged to the National Wholesale Hardware Association, based in Philadelphia, and managed by a professional association management firm, Fernley & Fernley. Tom Fernley, Jr., was the association's secretary for decades and was succeeded in the postwar period by his son, Tom III, known as T 3. Dealer-owned firms were not allowed to join the group for many years, however. That policy ultimately was changed.

Members of NWHA met annually each fall with members of the American Hardware Manufacturers Association, where the two groups networked and shared a common convention program.

As competition intensified, NWHA established an Industry Development Program to help its members and their retail customers cope with the increasing postwar competition. Seminars and workshops around the country were offered in this program.

Down south, another regional association served full line wholesalers—the Southern Wholesale Hardware Association, managed for many years in the postwar period by Ralph Kirby, who also was editor of *Southern Hardware* magazine. SWHA members met with AHMA members in the spring each year, similar to the NWHA-AHMA meeting.

And because the state was so large, Texas wholesalers formed their own association and met annually with manufacturing executives supplying them and with the manufacturers' reps traveling Texas, representing the hundreds of factories that did not have their own sales forces.

Today NWHA and SWHA no longer exist, and the 44 wholesalers who once operated in Texas are down to 6 firms, but there still is a Texas Wholesale Hardware Association.

Chapter Eight

THE ROLE OF ASSOCIATIONS AND TRADE MAGAZINES

It's been said of Americans that if a dozen of them get together and find they share a common interest in something, they'll form an association. And once an association is formed and the new activity is properly identified, it's likely a trade magazine will be developed to serve that group or industry. There are reported to be 7,600 associations in the U.S. today.

The hardware/home center industry has been served, over the years, by a number of associations and trade magazines. As times changed and competition eliminated many retailers and wholesalers, it also decimated the number of trade magazines and depleted the ranks of the industry's trade associations.

Each level of the industry has had its own associations—manufacturing, wholesaling and retailing. The energy and vision of the leaders of the various associations varied over time, ranging from caretaker to change-maker.

Probably no association executive changed the entire industry more than Russell R. Mueller, who became Managing Director of the National Retail Hardware Association in the early 1950s. NRHA, as it is commonly referred to in the hardware industry, was formed at the turn of the century and for many years had been managed by a man named Rivers Peterson, a capable but not inspiring association executive.

When he retired, the board picked Russ Mueller, then head of the New England Retail Hardware Association, to replace him. What they got was a dynamic, charismatic, talented super-salesman filled with visions of what NRHA should do and what the industry could become.

He envisioned and brought to life a united industry, working with manufacturers, wholesalers and retailers in promoting their products to the American consumer. He also greatly enlarged NRHA'S staff, brought new talent on board, provided a more liberal budget to its trade magazine, Hardware Retailer, and enlarged and improved upon existing NRHA services and activities.

Under his management, NRHA became the research center for the industry, changing that department from one that simply recorded cost-of-doing-business information into one that studied the entire industry and sought ways to improve its performance. The research department began providing market research for manufacturers, studied wholesaling and analyzed retailing in order to help members grow and thrive.

Recognizing needs was a Mueller specialty. He realized that the success of independent retailers, whether hardware store or lumber/building material dealer, depended on the knowledge and quality of their employees, yet that important—yes, vital—task of training and educating the nation's store employees was being left to chance.

Early on, he identified 8 basic industry needs:

More store traffic
More sales
Increased profits
Better trained personnel
Modern merchandising
More promotions
Improved competitive position
Better communications

To solve one problem, he dedicated NRHA to produce a comprehensive educational program and product, the Advanced Course in Hardware Retailing. ACHR became a series of departmental text books employees could study at home, be graded upon, be rewarded for their successful completion and even be recognized at both store and industry level. From that textbook beginning, NRHA's educational efforts expanded to include a series of training films, training seminars around the nation and other educational services. All made available at minimal cost to NRHA members and, when appropriate, to the nation's manufacturers and wholesalers, too.

But nothing impacted the industry quite as much as Mueller's development of coordinated national promotions uniting all three levels of hardware distribution—manufacturer, wholesaler and retailer. While NRHA had promoted an idea called "Hardware Week" for years prior to his arrival in Indianapolis, it was Mueller who made it and subsequent themes nationally powerful events. Consumer sweepstakes were part of the national advertising package. Prizes included such things as…European trips, cruises, vacation packages including lodging at condominiums, as well as automobiles—all designed to bring traffic into the stores. Twice a year, millions of shoppers frequented participating retailers during these events.

Long before there was any other organized national advertising for the industry and its retailers, NRHA paved the way for later wholesaling efforts to promote the services and products offered by independent retailers such as those now promoting True Value, Ace Hardware, Trustworthy stores and others.

He established a new NRHA department, Industry Activities, and brought in new people to staff it, particularly Richard H. (Rick) Lambert, who later became NRHA's Managing Director. Mueller himself was, perhaps, the industry's most effective salesman in convincing manufacturers to allocate tens—and even hundreds— of thousands of dollars to support coordinated marketing efforts through the hardware industry.

NRHA produced in-store decorative kits, ran ads in major national magazines, provided radio spots and later TV support for additional publicity. Every possible effort was made to bring into one common effort support for these promotions. Wholesaler sales meetings were addressed; store decorative art was supplied so wholesalers' own store decorative kits tied in with the NRHA promotional themes.

To improve the industry's stature with consumers, a nationwide PR campaign was launched and a new symbol developed, the "Handy Helpful Hardwareman™."

The results of these efforts, which lasted for several decades, even after Mueller's death, were a united industry that kept the American public convinced that independent and small chain retailing was an important, friendly, qualified place to shop for hardware and lumber/building material products.

He moved NRHA into still another activity. Store improvement and modernization had been a service initiated by some state and regional affiliated hardware associations for decades, but it had never been organized and coordinated at a national level. Mueller solved that problem and created the Master Merchant™ department, which developed an exclusive line of store fixtures and systematized the modernization efforts of the affiliated association personnel with regular training sessions, a consistent advertising program in *Hardware Retailing*, and continued editorial support for modernization activities of individual members.

NRHA under Mueller wanted to be sure that the American consumer would find hardware stores and lumber/building material dealers the preferred place to buy the products needed to repaint, repair and restore their homes and lawns.

Mueller truly believed in a coordinated, cooperative industry and for many activities formed advisory councils consisting of manufacturers and wholesalers as well as NRHA staff and retailers.

One of its more unusual programs was a series of seminars held in 22 cities across the nation, called *Cavalcade for Profits*, emphasizing cooperation, marketing and research to benefit all three distribution levels. In a sense these were continued, in somewhat different form by the association's magazine, *Hardware Retailing*, as described later.

NRHA had no direct retail members of its own. Retailers joined one of the nearly three dozen state and regional associations which comprised NRHA. Interestingly, NRHA's dues income was 50 cents a member, plus $1.00 per store for its subscription to *Hardware Retailing* magazine. Obviously, other sources of revenue were needed to finance the expansion of staff which occurred under Mueller.

The programs he began were continued and expanded under William G. (Bill) Mashaw, who succeeded Mueller after his untimely death in 1967 from cancer at the age of 55. In recognition of Mueller's leadership and dedication to the industry, the Russell R. Mueller Retail Hardware Research Foundation was launched in 1968, funded by all 3 levels of the industry. It continues to this day and the research it has conducted has helped the industry in many ways.

When home centers began to become a dominant segment of the retailing community, NRHA formed the Home Center Institute, so it could bring in these larger firms as direct members and prevent another association being formed to serve them. NRHA also recognized that these larger stores needed some different services than the average, much smaller individual hardware store or lumber dealer, though in the development of HCI programs, smaller member retailers would also be able to benefit through their usage.

One service developed for home centers, but also made available to all other NRHA members, was a series of "Show-How™" pamphlets—instruction sheets for dozens of home improvement and repair tasks, which retailers could imprint with their own names and provide to customers.

The state and regional hardware associations varied in size and services, depending upon the talents and dedication of its operation officers. Some were very aggressive and ambitious, others were content to work legislatively and be more passive. Store modernization came to be a mainstay of member services among many of NRHA's affiliated associations, primarily due to the efforts of C. J. (Chris) Christopher of the Minnesota Retail Hardware Association. Working with a local fixture manufacturer, the Streater company, the Minnesota association developed a line of store fixtures ideally suited to make a hardware retailer's sales floor more efficient. These then became available through all the other associations so retailers all around the country had access to modern fixtures.

Replacing old style flat-top fixtures with their limited display capability or sometimes ugly home-made fixtures, the association's display tables provided retailers with 3 display levels, with the widest display area at the bottom and narrower displays on the next two levels. Some had closed bottom shelves, providing reserve-stock storage space or security for merchandise. These served the industry for many years, until gondola fixtures came into being, along with the advent of perfboard and later, slot walls.

Another service offered by many of the affiliated associations was professional accounting and tax preparation. Specializing as they did, association accountants not only helped retailers "keep books" but they offered advice to help retailers improve their performance. These later developed into computerized accounting services for members. Helping members save money, associations offered group insurance programs that reduced premium costs substantially.

Out of these efforts came NRHA's annual Cost-of-Doing-Business reports for hardware stores and later, lumber/building material dealers and home centers. These continue to exist and provide the industry its only authentic guide to improved retail management. These are made available to every member at no charge.

For both store modernization and accounting services under Mueller, NRHA brought association personnel providing these services into Indianapolis for training and idea exchanges on an annual basis.

The last two decades have not been kind to state and regional hardware associations. As wholesalers began providing many of the services once offered by the associations, income sources disappeared and staffs had to be reduced and then fewer services could be offered. Membership also declined as stores went out of business or retailers decided to simply rely completely on their wholesalers.

As a result, NRHA's affiliated state and regional associations began to disappear. At one time, there were 37. By 1992, there were only 14 remaining. NRHA not too much later began having its own financial problems. Most of its income came from the services and programs it developed for the benefit of manufacturers and the advertising revenue from its magazine. The association's magazine, *Hardware Retailing* (then changed to *Do It Yourself Retailing*) began losing advertising revenue, as did the other trade magazines serving the industry.

Wholesalers sought manufacturer ad dollars for their own marketing programs and thus the industry-wide NRHA promotional programs ultimately disappeared.

The result was that NRHA suffered its own problems, and it wasn't until John Hammond became Managing Director in 1994 that things began to be turned around. Hammond's first—and biggest—task was to bring it back from the brink, seeing to it that NRHA would survive to serve the next generation of retailers.

To generate revenue in a declining advertising market, he took NRHA into the "Custom Publishing" arena. In an environment where powerful wholesalers and large retailers were extracting more promotional dollars from manufacturers—at the expense of the industry's trade magazines—the association created custom magazines that let wholesalers, large retailers and manufacturers communicate directly with their customers. NRHA has produced as many as 11 specialty magazines at one time. The development of this new department within NRHA provided it with a much expanded means of communicating with retailers on "how-to" management and merchandising issues. Custom publishing remains an important service NRHA continues to provide to all levels of the industry.

As noted before, NRHA had been getting only $.50 per member in dues income per retailer from its affiliated associations. By developing a Direct Membership Region concept, NRHA assumed management of state and regional associations as they fell upon difficult financial times. Over a period of years, it finally resulted in a truly national association—a direct connection between NRHA and its retail membership base.

When the affiliated Canadian Retail Hardware Association ceased to exist, NRHA brought Canadian members into the organization as direct members, leading to its name change to North American Retail Hardware Association, enabling it to keep the now-familiar NRHA identity.

Just as wholesaling (and to some extent retailing) had moved from a series of small, local supply chains to nationwide wholesale distribution networks and national retail programs, so too did NRHA evolve.

NRHA then began to implement "wholesale group memberships". It implemented group membership packages for every member retailer at True Value, Ace Hardware and Canada's Home Hardware. Later, smaller, custom group membership programs were created for other distributors, both in the U. S. and Canada.

Advances in technology also played a role in NRHA's revival. It opened the door to high volume grading of the Advanced Course in Hardware Retailing through computer scanning and allowed the program to be offered to the industry's large chain members, most of whom belonged to the Home Center Institute, the group-within-a-group formed by NRHA when home centers first emerged as a distinct class of retailers within the hardware industry. Wholesale groups also could now offer the Advanced Course in Hardware Retailing to their retailers, helping to insure the qualified, trained salespeople which help their retailers distinguish themselves from competition.

With the advent of the Internet, that program became entirely electronic and makes it possible to educate tens of thousands of retail employees in a cost-effective and profitable fashion.

NRHA's move into electronic communication with retailers is rapidly expanding under the leadership of NRHA's current Managing Director, Bill Lee. Hammond retired at the end of 2008.

At the manufacturing level

There were—and still are—a number of associations serving the hardware industry's manufacturers. Two are industry-wide, others serve specific segments of the manufacturing community.

For more than 100 years, the hardware/home improvement industry has benefited from trade associations serving the nation's manufacturers. Many trade associations serve specific segments of the manufacturing community while the American Hardware Manufacturers Association (AHMA) has served and continues to serve the entire industry.

Segment-specific associations include those focused on product categories. The largest and most prominent of these is the International Housewares Association (IHA), formerly known as the National Housewares Manufacturers Association. Others serve manufacturers of builders hardware, sporting goods, hand tools, power tools, safety and security, lawn and garden and many other products.

American Hardware Manufacturers Association

AHMA, organized in 1901, has always been recognized as an industry-wide association serving manufacturers of products in all categories. Sixty-seven companies signed on as charter members and the association was headquartered in Cleveland.   For many years, AHMA focused its attention on member services with modest legislative activity and annual meetings with members of the National Wholesale Hardware Association and the Southern Wholesale Hardware Association.

Activities at AHMA ramped up in 1972 when Charles Spencer, then president of Skil Corp., was elected AHMA president. Spencer wanted AHMA to become officially involved in the National Hardware Show®. It was a natural fit because its members were exhibitors at the show, which was founded in 1946 by Charles Snitow.

The AHMA board appointed a committee to develop a Hardware Industry Week™ that would incorporate a trade show. The committee was composed of industry veterans including soon-to-be AHMA executive officer William P. (Bill) Farrell, then editor and publication director of *Hardware Merchandiser* magazine.   Spencer, with the backing of the AHMA board and on the advice of the Committee, convinced Snitow that he should invite AHMA to participate in the National Hardware Show®, instead of facing the prospect of competing with an AHMA-sponsored show.

By 1977, the Hardware Show and AHMA had moved to Chicago and AHMA was sponsoring and conducting the show, using Snitow's company as the show manager. AHMA sponsored and conducted the National Hardware Show® in Chicago for more than 25 years.

In 1980, after several short-term executives, the board hired Farrell to be its executive officer. The AHMA board of directors felt that Farrell's participation in securing AHMA's interest in the Show, combined with his 20-plus years' publication experience, equipped him to oversee the association's interest in the show as well as all other facets of operating the association.   Under his leadership, the association began expanding member programs and services as well as financing industry projects to benefit not only its members but the wholesalers and retailers who were the customers of its members.

AHMA invested the income from the National Hardware Show® back into the industry in the form of a growing assortment of programs, services and activities. Farrell formed a "Participating Associations" group to assist with selecting topics for presentation at the annual Show event held in August in Chicago. These included the NRHA, National Wholesale Hardware Association, Southern Wholesale Hardware Association, Builders Hardware Manufacturers Association, Hand Tools Institute, National Lumber & Building Materials Association, Lawn & Garden Marketing and Distribution Association, North American Building Material Distribution Association and the North American Wholesale Lumber Association.

Among its other activities was the development of AHMA/USA pavilions at international trade shows in foreign countries to help member firms develop export business—up to 10 international pavilions in some years in Europe, Asia, South America and Mexico. It was in 1982 that the association launched its first and biggest international pavilion—at the International Hardware Fair in Cologne, Germany. Those pavilions, a variety of conferences it conducted, co-sponsoring two annual national conventions with distribution and other assorted activities, also contributed income to AHMA's coffers so it could enhance activities benefiting the industry.

With the income from the National Hardware Show® and other service activities, AHMA began offering many new industry-wide programs. During Hardware Industry Week™, held in conjunction with the National Hardware Show®, educational seminars covered virtually every management topic of concern to retailers, wholesalers and industry manufacturers. Headline speakers ranged from former presidents of the United States, foreign heads of state, members of Congress to presidents of the biggest retail chains and organizations in the industry, including top foreign speakers such as Manfred Maus, who at the time headed up one of Europe's largest suppliers of hardware, building supplies and home improvement products throughout Europe

Under Farrell's management, the AHMA invested significant time and resources developing a computerized order-entry program for its members and their customers called The Eagle System, which was operated under a separate corporation from AHMA known as American Hardware Data Systems, Inc., which Farrell headed as Chief Operating Officer. Once up and running and proven successful, the AHMA transferred its interest in the program to Sterling Software, which offered the program to the industry until new technology changed the course of that function.

Farrell, with his background in communications, quickly pursued a two-pronged strategy: improve and enhance the organization's program offerings, and boost its image and visibility, both domestically and internationally.

A Young Executives Council was formed to involve up-and-coming younger men and women in the association and help them begin to form networking friendships that would benefit both them and the industry.

It was way back in 1991 that the association sponsored its first Technology Conference, a meeting that continues annually to this day, now known as the Hardlines Technology Forum™, though the kinds of discussions taking place today are far removed from the kinds of "technology" discussed nearly two decades ago.

Thirty years ago, another much smaller association was formed when 5 AHMA members exhibiting at the International Hardware Fair in Cologne, Germany, decided it would be helpful if an organization was formed to help member companies become more knowledgeable about opportunities and considerations needed to expand international sales. They called it the Worldwide DIY Council.

Today it continues to exist with an expanded array of services—including a monthly newsletter, staging group pavilions in smaller shows around the world, holding meetings overseas and visiting stores in international markets, and conducting table-top shows in conjunction with its international meetings. Its web site lists members in a variety of ways, including the kinds of products each member makes, and provides a news page of information about international trade shows, key retailers and wholesalers around the world and other items of international interest to site visitors.

Still another broad-based association, organized in 1971, is the Hardware Marketing Council, a limited group of senior marketing and sales executives who meet twice each year to exchange ideas and network.

The International Housewares Association

Much like the American Hardware Manufacturers Association, the industry's housewares association transformed itself over the years. For many postwar years, its primary activity was conducting two large trade shows a year. Times changed, and the industry needed only one such show a year. Times continued to change, and the association realized its members had other needs, and it began providing other services.

IHA continues to conduct an international housewares show which attracts buyers from all channels of distribution as well as from many foreign countries, in addition to those from the U. S. It also provides prime lobby display space to promote packaging improvements, showcases new products, and conducts seminars on a variety of merchandising, management and promotional topics to assist show attendees improve their businesses.

Other expanded services for IHA now include an ongoing research program and expanded public relations program about housewares trends at the consumer level, special educational meetings as well as keeping member firms up to date on legislative matters.

One of its most successful service additions has been the formation of the Housewares Export Council of North American (HECNA), whose goal it is to help members sell internationally. Since HECNA was formed, it has conducted meetings at which it brings in international retailers to discuss their businesses with HECNA members, thus enabling the members to establish personal relationships with key business prospects as well as to better understand those retailers and the countries in which they are operating.

HECNA also now sponsors group pavilions in some international trade shows, providing members with low-cost display facilities which offer the added bonus of a more impressive "group" presentation.

Associations serving wholesalers

Today, the major associations which served hardware wholesalers for decades no longer exist. They, like many of their once-member firms, are out of business. The major association for wholesalers was the National Wholesale

Hardware Association (NWHA), managed for decades by a professional association-management firm based in Philadelphia, Fernley & Fernley. Tom Fernley, Jr. was the NWHA manager for several decades and was followed by his son, known as T 3.

NWHA members met annually with members of the American Hardware Manufacturers Association every fall and AHMA members met in the spring with members of the Southern Wholesale Hardware Association. The Southern Wholesale Hardware Association was managed for many years by Ralph Kirby, also editor of *Southern Hardware* magazine. He retired and the association no longer exists, nor does the magazine.

As wholesalers went out of business, membership dropped for both organizations, and finally, the two associations ended their individual existence. In 1993, wholesale associations merged to form the International Hardware Distributors Group, and in 2000 it consolidated with the North American Building Material Distributors Association and formed an organization known as Wholesale Hardware Distribution Alliance, but it too no longer exists.

Interestingly, one small wholesalers' association continues to exist—the Texas Wholesale Hardware Association. Once there were 44 wholesale members of the group operating in Texas, but today there are only 6 wholesalers remaining in the state, but the association continues.

Trade magazines serving the industry

Trade magazines play a vital role in almost every American industry—reporting on what is happening, forecasting what might happen and profiling the companies and individuals comprising it. Their new-product sections enable new manufacturers to enter the marketplace and help retailers find interesting, useful new products to offer their customers and to distinguish their merchandise offerings from those of competitors.

The hardware industry was no different, and for many postwar years was served by quite a number of trade magazines, some regional and some national. At various times there were between 6 and 9 trade magazines in the industry.

Today, however, there are only two hardware magazines left—the one owned and published by the North American Retail Hardware Association, and the other by Lebhar-Friedman, a New York-based, privately-owned publishing company. The decimation was even greater among publications serving the lumber/building material trade. None survived.

The magazines in the industry tried to change as the industry changed, but most did not succeed. The oldest publication in the industry was *Hardware Age,* founded in the mid 1800s and for many years owned by The Chilton Co., a Philadelphia-based publisher of a whole array of trade magazines.

NRHA's magazine, originally called *Hardware Retailer*, came into existence shortly after NRHA was formed at the turn of the century. In the postwar period, it first changed its name slightly to *Hardware Retailing*, recognizing that its audience consisted of several types of retailers selling hardware, such as lumber/building material dealers and the emerging home center retailers.

Later, as the Do It Yourself movement gained momentum, the magazine changed its name to *Do It Yourself Retailing.* But it reverted back to *Hardware Retailing* in 2008.

As an association publication and reflecting NRHA's desire to serve the entire industry for the ultimate benefit of its retail members, *Hardware Retailing* for many years conducted a dozen or more free seminars every fall all around the country for manufacturers' sales and marketing executives and for the advertising agencies serving those firms.

What was most unusual about these meetings was that they were non-commercial. In other words, they were not "media presentations", but rather were objective reports on the market—its size, the major players in the field, major trends taking place, etc.—the kinds of information manufacturers and advertising personnel needed to make informed decisions as to how best meet the needs of the industry's wholesalers and retailers.

In the lumber/building material industry, there were two major publications—*Building Supply News* and *American Lumberman*. The latter, as the secondary publication in the market, changed its name to *Home Center* in an effort to rejuvenate its advertising income and circulation as home centers began attracting so much manufacturer attention. The magazine even developed a Home Center trade show, which existed successfully for several years before most of the business began to be concentrated in the fantastic growth of Home Depot and Lowe's and the smaller home center chains began dying off.

The early growth and importance of home centers also captured the attention of Lebhar-Friedman executives, who launched *National Home Center News*, a tabloid publication out of New York. It too has changed its name, becoming *Home Channel News* in recognition of the fact that the home center industry today is dominated by three chains—Home Depot, Lowe's and Menards—and it needed to serve a wider audience. Buying decisions are intensely concentrated, so trade advertising in that field by manufacturers is no longer as effective. As smaller home center chains went out of business, circulation numbers decreased. The market simply became more concentrated.

By changing its name and coverage to now include other types of stores selling hardware and lumber/building material products, it felt that it would have a better chance of convincing manufacturers to advertise in it. The magazine recently began publishing less frequently and now is a conventional magazine size, having abandoned its tabloid format.

Chapter Nine

THE COMPUTER AGE

In the late 1950s and early 1960's, the hardware industry—at all levels—changed dramatically.

The computer age in merchandising was born.

Suddenly a means became available that would enable wholesalers to grow into multi-billion dollar distribution systems. . . that would enable manufacturers to improve their products and production processes. . . that would enable retailers to identify fast-sellers as well as slow or no-sellers and improve their returns on investment and stock turns.

Well, truth be told, it didn't happen suddenly, but it did happen as the years went by. . . as computers became smaller but infinitely more powerful and simpler to use . . . and as people at all levels discovered new ways to unleash the magic computers represented.

Punch card computing came first, and automated some systems, but it wasn't until IBM developed the 360 computer that wholesalers were able to devise new ways to use them and improve their own operations. Who would have envisioned way back then that individuals would own their own computers—not just one per household, but sometimes two or three, and that students would be carrying to school laptop computers with nearly as much or more computing power than those being operated by some of the largest wholesalers of the time?

In a landmark report in October of 1968, *Hardware Retailer* magazine devoted 64 pages to a comprehensive study of computers at work at all levels of the industry called "The computer age in merchandising." The study concluded by prophesying "The computer age in merchandising will be an exciting—and profitable—era. It will have problems, but the rewards should far overshadow the problems."

Hardware wholesalers, back in the early stages of computerization, led almost all other types of distribution in devising innovative ways to put computers to work. They certainly led manufacturers in their use and, because they were far bigger with more resources, were far ahead of retailing's adoption of computerization.

While manufacturers needed to control the production and distribution of a few hundred or a few thousand items, wholesalers were and still are faced with the challenge of managing the distribution of 20,000 to 60,000 items. Retailers, unfortunately, always faced somewhat similar problems, and fortunately, over time, specialized software companies developed systems to help retailers cope with those problems.

Today's largest wholesalers, serving thousands of retailers, would not be able to handle that kind of business without today's computers.

In the early postwar years, small wholesalers were able to compete with larger wholesalers because decision-making largely rested on the talents of its people—buyers making buying decisions on what to stock, when to re-buy, and when to change sources or drop items. When computers began to automate some of the re-buying functions, larger wholesalers, better able to finance computerization, began to gain against their smaller competitors. Time-sharing and service bureaus evolved to solve the problems facing smaller wholesalers, and as computers dropped in price so dramatically, those kinds of problems gradually disappeared and the playing field became more level once again.

In its 1968 in-depth study of computers, *Hardware Retailer* worked closely with and studied computer usage in 14 wholesale firms, as well as with a number of manufacturers. Just how competitive and challenging the postwar era has been is proven when one realizes that only 5 of those large wholesalers (at that time) remain in business. Others were acquired or went out of business.

Wholesalers put computers to use in 5 areas:

§ operational
§ financial
§ purchasing
§ sales
§ dealer services.

Some wholesalers floundered a bit in the early days of The Computer Age by trying to do too much too fast. One early problem was learning how to manage by exception—not to get all the reports a computer could generate telling you what happened but to learn to rely only on those reports which identified problems that needed correction.

Today, with computers so tiny and so powerful that one's cell phone or Blackberry has as much or more capacity than some of the very earliest computers, it is hard to imagine the problems early adopters faced in the 1960s. They faced resistance among their employees. . . they tried to do too much too fast and boggled and bumbled. . . they became inundated with too many reports. . . but they solved them all and the survivors ended up as larger, more successful firms.

Buyers were able to determine, more easily, which products and which brands deserved more of their investment. As retailers adopted computerization, they too learned the same lessons. Accounts could be analyzed and, if unprofitable, either dropped or upgraded to profitability.

Computers were—and are—used to measure the performance of personnel, whether warehouse staff, office staff, sales people. Invoicing became faster and automated; aging and collecting accounts became simpler; statements became automated; return-on-investment improved (for the survivors) and "outs" became less of a problem. Today a number of wholesalers claim they are shipping 97% of orders received. Sales could be analyzed by vendor, by sales person, and by retailer. Commission reports became automatic.

One area where computers were put to early use by wholesalers was in the area of dealer services. Computer-printed bin tickets became a godsend to retailers. Now they could identify homes for merchandise in their

Computers sort products by dealer orders and vastly improve distribution center efficiencies in so many different ways.

stores, and as prices changed, so could their bin tickets to keep these loca-tions up to date. Best of all, perhaps, were the price stickers wholesalers began providing, so that items could be ticketed and put on shelves ready to be sold—in hours instead of days. It also became possible for dealers to have personalized pricing with these computer-generated stickers.

Wholesalers helped retailers by providing guidance about suggested retail prices and began reporting overall and departmental margins to their customers.

Computers were put to use to help wholesalers in their own opera-tions, too, of course. And in many different ways.

They were used to analyze sales by item and line and mathematically computed the proper bin sizes in warehouses to make maximum use of available space. Those analyses were made based on the physical size of items, by sales volume, average inventory, frequency of orders shipped and size and frequency of incoming shipments. Such information made them infinitely more efficient in their distribution centers and kept their operat-ing costs down so their retailers could remain competitive in the market-place.

They also were used to re-plan warehouses based on physical charac-teristics of merchandise, instead of by traditional merchandise categories. Without computers, there would be none of the automated warehousing now found at both the manufacturing and wholesaling levels.

Computers led to the streamlining of inventories. Slow-movers were more readily identified and dropped, improving return-on-investment. Re-buying became more automated, and freed buyers from the tedium of record-keeping, theoretically giving them time to be better merchants. Admittedly, this sometimes was (and remains) only a theory.

Best of all, from a retailer's standpoint, order-fill percentages began increasing and now attain standards never before possible.

Internally, computers enabled wholesalers to monitor gross margins by buyer, by department, by vendor. Line-billing values could be reviewed. Cash-flows improved.

Computers helped wholesalers identify "problem accounts", such as dealers who abused return-goods or caused credit problems. The more computers were adopted, the more innovative were the applications wholesalers devised.

In the late '60s, wholesalers using computers realized that these were the tools that would enable them to know the profitability of individual lines, customers and vendors. The computer age was here.

Before computerization became affordable and available for the average hardware or lumber/building material retailer, wholesalers began using their own computers to help customers. They began providing purchase reports to their customers, which provided monthly reports on purchases, inventory at cost and suggested retail, margins and profits, and monthly, quarterly and year-to-date sales and gross profits realized. Such reports began to provide retailers with information during the year that never before had been available.

In the early days of computer adoption by wholesalers, some became deeply committed to putting computers to work in the dealer-service area. Others did little at first. That changed as retailers embraced the offerings of competitive firms.

Here are some of the early ways in which wholesalers used their computers to help customers:

Helping retailers buy more intelligently
Helping retailers sell
Helping retailers receive and price goods
Helping retailers improve stockturns and reduce outs
Helping retailers improve margins
Helping retailers departmentalize their stores
Helping retailers become better businessmen and managers
Helping retailers promote more intelligently and with better results
Helping retailers with their accounting and financial management
Helping retailers take inventory
Helping new owners get into the business by advising on basic stocks, quantities, etc.

While wholesalers suggested retail prices for products, a process that is ongoing even now, quite often little genuine research was behind the price-setting, a complaint one continues to hear from retailers to this date. Dealers say that some items are not priced competitively enough, but more often, the concern is that margins are unnecessarily low and profits are needlessly given away.

To remedy these shortcomings, wholesalers began providing retailers with the opportunity to determine their own pricing on bin tickets and price stickers. One of the first wholesalers to offer this service was Hardware Wholesalers, Inc., now Do it Best Corp.

By analyzing sales and repeat orders for items appearing in their consumer direct-mail circulars and catalogs, wholesalers also have been able to improve the performance of these retail sales aids. Co-op ad allowances still play a part in item selection, as does product seasonality, but the computer-generated data about actual sales discourages repeats of slow-sellers.

Computers also make possible evaluation of repeat items being promoted at various price-points. Surprisingly, studies show that it is not always the lowest price that promotes the greatest sales.

Hardware and lumber/building material retailers always have coped with the problems inherent in their stocking so many items. Many used to try to manage their business by having only one department—the store—but as computerization began to spread into retailing, cash registers, then point-of-sale terminals and computers began offering 4 and then 8 and finally far more departmental breakdowns to record sales, and wholesale purchase reports provided records about buys.

Today computerization at retail is at the item level, thanks to software providers like Activant and RockSolid, to name just two of a number of providers who are offering turnkey systems which retailers are using to manage every aspect of their businesses, especially rates of sale.

In the late 1960s, wholesalers realized that the chain competition their customers faced was moving quickly towards "total systems" that would provide detailed information on product movement. They recognized that they needed to work together with their customer base to match the

With laptops, retailers are taking computers onto the sales floor to check stock and pricing.

programs and concepts being used by chain competition. It has been an ongoing process over the decades since.

Back in 1968, *Hardware Retailer* surveyed wholesalers of all sizes to find out how many were using computers and how they were being used. At that time, half were computerized. As wholesalers headed into the next decade, it was "computerize or die."

One interesting fact from that long-ago research was the tiny size of wholesalers way back then. The average volume of reporting firms using computers in 1968 was $13.5 million; those NOT using computers, $2.8 million. Today, even small specialty wholesalers are doing far more than some of these figures. And it is not at all uncommon to find independently owned hardware stores, home centers and lumber/building material retailers doing that much or more. That study, at the time, included most of the industry's largest distributors.

Obviously, wholesalers sought to improve their own operations via computer, and they did so by focusing first on purchasing and sales efforts. "Outs" reports helped improve order-filling, along with stock-status reports. Computer link-ups with vendors were just beginning in the late '60s. Today they are commonplace.

From a sales standpoint, customer analysis was a basic computer use, together with salesperson analysis. Direct mail analysis began to be more widely used. Reviews of merchandise by department and fine-line class became possible.

Catalogs became easier to produce and keep up to date. With most wholesalers stocking 20,000 or more items, catalog preparation had always been a tough and expensive task for distributors.

The manufacturer's use of computers

Manufacturers were quicker to adopt the use of computers than retailers or wholesalers, in part because it was easier for them to do so. They weren't trying to manage tens of thousands of SKUs, buy from hundreds of vendors or sell to thousands of customers. Much like wholesalers, manufacturers began utilizing computers for customer and salesperson analysis, as well as cost analysis in the production of products. Like wholesalers, too, they used computers to improve their warehousing and distribution processes. And in the late 60s they were just beginning to link up with their customers' computers.

The years since have only served to enhance and improve all those processes.

Computerization at retail

When one looks back at hardware/home center retailing, one realizes that computerization became a necessity, not just for large stores but for all stores. Retailers were carrying so many items that they needed to better manage their inventories, get rid of dead items, increase stocks of better sellers, price some items competitively and increase margins on blind items if they wanted to survive.

Only a computer could make those goals a practical reality.

Retailers in the postwar years first began to departmentalize their stores, recognizing that that one department—the store—simply wasn't adequate. But doing this manually was terribly time-consuming, and for many retailers, just too much work. Departmental registers helped solve the problem but did not provide the details that computers and more sophisticated point-of-sale terminals could.

Retailers now can track sales by item and thus improve stockturns while still better serving their communities and customers.

At retail, computers and the reports they and the systems provide did—and continue to—transform retailing by helping retailers to:

Expand departments when sales are shown to be growing
Reduce space allocated to those with declining sales
Evaluate effectiveness of advertising on an item-basis
Evaluate effectiveness of advertising based on item pricing
Reduce the time needed to buy
Reduce the time needed to receive and restock merchandise
Provide guidance for trips to a wholesaler's buying market or trade show

While the big chains certainly have a financial advantage in terms of being able to fund investment in the technology infrastructure required today, software providers keep improving their complete store systems, which give smaller retailers the same kinds of information needed for smart decision-making.

As one industry observer noted recently, "Historically, as retailing came to rely on technology to realize supply chain efficiencies and make store-level operations more effective, smaller retailers became increasingly disadvantaged. This was compounded by national brands' increasing focus on the largest ten or fifteen retailers who drove most of their revenue, and to a great extent ignoring smaller retailers and even regional chains who simply could not move the needle for a national brand."

Today technology providers realize there is opportunity to provide sophisticated solutions to smaller retailers using a Software-as-a-Service (SaaS) model. Things like price optimization and pricing systems are now available to smaller retailers. Even sophisticated loyalty solutions are being made available such as Retalix's for smaller retailers in the StoreNext network.

While larger retailers, especially the chains, are now using loyalty cards, another way in which computers are being put to use, smaller retailers who are essentially closer to their customers are better able to build relationships with their shoppers using loyalty systems. And, as smaller retailers begin to truly understand their business in terms of shoppers, they are able to more quickly and aggressively shift their priorities and investments to align with the opportunities than larger companies can.

Once again, the computer helps out.

Chapter Ten

SHOWS—AND MORE SHOWS

No one seems to know for sure when the very first show was held for hardware store owners so they could evaluate the products and promotions offered by producers of the tens of thousands of products stocked by the typical store, but given the tremendous breadth of inventory a store stocks, someone early on figured out that an exhibition was necessary so retailers could check out "what's new" and examine competitive products to make the right buying decision.

For many years before the war and after World War II, state and regional hardware associations conducted annual shows. The shows were a major income source for these associations, and were supported by local wholesalers in most instances. The shows gave manufacturers an opportunity to show their wares and to learn firsthand what retailers and wholesalers were thinking.

But times changed. Wholesalers began developing store programs in which retailers were identified by a common name associated with the wholesaler—either as a dealer-owned firm (True Value, for example) or with a privately owned firm promoting a program—Pro, for another example. Some wholesalers, of course, had conducted their own shows (or markets, as many came to be known) while associations also conducted shows.

It wasn't long before more wholesalers began holding their own buying events, often calling them "markets". Soon, faced with a decision as to which shows to support, manufacturers chose the wholesaler markets because they felt more buying would take place there. And that spelled the end of association-sponsored trade shows and, financially, was an instrumental factor in the operating troubles that began affecting state and regional hardware associations. A major income source disappeared.

The transition from association shows to wholesaler markets took place over about a 10 year period, with some associations hanging on desperately to their own shows, but finally, they all disappeared.

Today, many wholesalers conduct two markets a year, giving retailers an opportunity to buy seasonal goods as well as to replace basic stocks with special show-special pricing. Wholesalers also now use shows as educational events for their affiliated retailers, conducting training sessions of many kinds and bringing in inspirational speakers to "charge up" retailers for the competitive battles they'll face in their own trading areas.

Buyers work closely with exhibiting manufacturers in developing special buys that will encourage the maximum amount of buying for vendors (and wholesalers) and offer attending retailers some extra margins.

New items get a lot of featured treatment, and wholesaler shows offer new vendors an opportunity to break into the hardware/home center business enthusiastically and successfully. Millions of dollars of buying now take place over a few days in some of these wholesaler-sponsored buying extravaganzas.

A national show emerges

Prior to World War II, there was no national show for retailers in the hardware/lumber/building material field. Everything was based on local areas—either the rare wholesaler show or the more common association-sponsored show.

But when the war ended, a lawyer and entrepreneur from New York City named Charles Snitow realized that there was huge pent-up demand for all the kinds of products hardware retailers and wholesalers would be stocking.   So in 1946, (Sept. 16-21) he opened the National Hardware Show® in the Grand Central Palace exhibit hall in Manhattan. One of his original exhibitors, General Tools & Equipment, continues to be a strong supporter of the show more than 60 years later.

A partial view of one section of the huge National Hardware Show®.

As the show grew and succeeded, it eventually moved to the New York Coliseum, a larger and better facility, and it remained there for many years before moving to the Midwest, where it occupied the McCormick Place exhibition facility on Chicago's Lake Michigan lake front, even-larger and more accessible to buyers in the Midwest and West, where more of the major wholesalers were located.

In an effort to aid the industry which was providing him such a wonderful income source, Snitow enthusiastically agreed, when approached in the early 60s by the Hardware/Housewares Packaging Committee of the Packaging Institute, to donate the use of the priceless lobby area of the Coliseum for a Packaging Exposition which would showcase innovations in packaging and merchandising displays. For a number of years, the Packaging Exposition, judged annually by a panel of well known retail and wholesale executives, highlighted the industry's ever-expanding packaging improvements and merchandising aids.

In the early 1970s, Snitow sold the show to Cahners Exposition Group, though he still maintained his connection with the show. It was about that time that the American Hardware Manufacturers Association, whose members were many of the show's largest exhibitors, decided the association should play a role with the show, a feeling that had been developing over the years as the show grew and became more and more successful.

In 1972, Skil Corp.'s president, Charles Spencer, was elected president of AHMA. He was committed to having AHMA play a role in the show's success and after some negotiations with the Reed Exposition Group, which had by then purchased the show from Cahners, AHMA began to sponsor and conduct the Hardware Industry Week™ educational program in connection with the show.

Using some of the funds generated for it by the ongoing Show, AHMA launched numerous programs, greatly expanded its service activities, and devoted itself to an ongoing educational program to benefit not only its members, but retailers and wholesalers as well.

After many years exhibiting in Chicago's McCormick Place, Reed Exhibitions decided to move the show to Las Vegas, a move which was objected to by the American Hardware Manufacturers Association, which had strong ties with Chicago. The result was a split between the two groups and AHMA is no longer participating in the show's revenue. Show management, however, is still conducting some educational activities in connection with the show, working now with the North American Retail Hardware Association.

Unable to get desired dates for one year after it moved to Las Vegas, the show took place in Florida that year, but now is permanently scheduled for Las Vegas.

The Show now includes special displays of "green products", new items and packaging—all efforts by show management to make it easier for buyers to keep up to date on emerging trends.

Today's National Hardware Show® is a huge event, with thousands of exhibitors, including hundreds of international vendors, often grouped by

*New products continue to be identified and featured in this special display
at the National Hardware Show®.*

their native country, and it attracts buyers from many channels of trade, not just hardware wholesalers and retailers—web-based retailers, mass merchandisers, drug and supermarket chains, dollar stores, etc.

Other national shows

Over the years, the National Hardware Show® came to be only one of a number of shows that would be of interest to retailers and wholesalers in the industry.

Because housewares was an important merchandise category for both wholesalers and retailers in the immediate postwar period, the Housewares Show, held twice a year for many years in Chicago and conducted by the National Housewares Manufacturers Association, played another important role in providing manufacturers with a showcase for their products, merchandising displays and promotions. It became less important to the hardware industry as wholesalers, and many retailers, shrunk or completely eliminated their housewares products. However, in the last few years, many retailers and some wholesalers are giving increased attention to the category once again and "shop the show".

Entrepreneurs and show management groups saw other opportunities to conduct shows featuring other product categories stocked by retailers and wholesalers, and shows were developed in the lawn and garden field, sporting goods, paints and sundries, and other categories. The automotive aftermarket spawned a number of shows because the market was so large.

As the home center industry began capturing the nation's attention in the 70s and 80s, George Milne, who was publisher of *American Lumberman* magazine, changed the name of the publication to *Home Center* and later conducted a Home Center Show for several years, but as the home center business began to be concentrated more and more among Home Depot and Lowe's, and so many pioneer home center chains disappeared from the retailing scene, the show too eventually disappeared, as did the magazine.

Today retailers can attend one or two markets a year sponsored by any wholesaler from whom they buy. . . .or other shows by other wholesalers serving their region. . . can attend specialty trade shows representing merchandise categories important for them. . . . or attend the two big national

Many retailers are showing renewed interest in housewares again and attend the International Housewares Show.

shows, the International Housewares Show® in Chicago or the National Hardware Show® in Las Vegas.

There is no shortage of shows today.

Chapter Eleven

INFLUENTIAL INDIVIDUALS IN THE INDUSTRY

The industry in the postwar period owes much of its growth—and, indeed, even its survival—to a relative handful of individuals who provided leadership, inspiration and vision to the men and women who ran manufacturing companies, wholesale businesses or retail establishments in the postwar period.

There undoubtedly are many more who deserve mention than the ones profiled here, but these, in the author's judgment, were probably the most influential and their accomplishments are briefly outlined here.

Russ Mueller

Russell R. Mueller, who headed the National Retail Hardware Association for many postwar years before his untimely death in 1967, probably did more than any other one person to revitalize the industry. He took over as NRHA's Managing Director in the early 1950s and converted NRHA from a traditional and rather laid-back retail association into a dynamic industry-changing force.

He expanded its staff, developed a research department and did many other things within the organization, but his most important accomplishment was to launch a series of industry-wide consumer promotions focusing the consumer's attention on hardware and lumber/building material retailers. The promotions were financed by industry manufacturers but included coordinated industry efforts by retailers and wholesalers, uniting a 3-level distribution system in a way in which none had ever been united before.

Thousands of retailers supported the promotions, as did hundreds of wholesalers and, over time, hundreds of manufacturers of a wide range of products. There were toy promotions, housewares promotions, lawn and garden promotions and the granddaddy of them all, Hardware Week promotions which included a wide range of products. Ads appeared in major consumer magazines and later ads appeared on television and radio stations urging Americans to shop at their neighborhood hardware stores or lumber/building material retailer.

Retailers were supplied point-of-sale store decorating kits; wholesalers supported the promotions with many millions of their own direct mail circulars and catalogs. It had never been done before in the hardware industry—and never on such a widespread scale in any industry.

Mueller was a charismatic man, impressive at a height of 6'4", with a booming voice. And a master salesman in person, who got his start as a "pitchman" at the Chicago World's Fair when he was a college student.

But he was more than a promoter of the industry. He recognized industry needs and committed NRHA's resources to solve them. For example, most retailers early in his NRHA days were not aggressively using credit as a sales tool, so NRHA developed a credit-selling manual and conducted seminars around the country, in most cases working through the affiliated state and regional associations which comprised NRHA.

Even more important, however, was his recognition that well trained, qualified salespeople in retail stores were essential if independent and small-chain retailers were to survive against large corporate chains. Thus was born the Advanced Course in Hardware Retailing, a comprehensive product knowledge educational program in which students could study departmental product manuals at home, at their own pace, and be granted recognition upon completion of the course. The program continues in modified and updated forms today. It was and is recognized and supported by wholesalers and manufacturers.

NRHA's educational efforts included development of training films about such subjects as curtailing shoplifting, creating better, more effective merchandise displays, etc. To keep costs low, NRHA staff doubled as actors and actresses, even portraying shoplifting customers at times. Type-casting, it was claimed, in some instances.

While NRHA had always provided a Cost-of-Doing-Business study to help its members compare their operations with industry averages, Mueller vastly expanded the association's research activities to include providing research services to manufacturers and wholesalers.

He brought in William G. (Bill) Mashaw from the FBI office in Washington, DC, to head up a new department which would work with manufacturers in establishing trade practices that would help, not harm, the industry.

He encouraged the addition of staff to the association's magazine, *Hardware Retailer*, and made sure it was "an industry magazine", not merely an association publication.

He brought industry executives to Indianapolis for working sessions on a variety of topics, and frequently entertained them at his own home. At the time, dealer-owned wholesalers were not recognized by the National Wholesale Hardware Association, but they were able to rub elbows with conventional wholesalers at NRHA and Mueller's home.

One of the services a number of the state and regional associations provided members was store modernization. Mueller hired experienced merchandising professionals and created a Master Merchant™ department to coordinate and train association personnel. People were brought to Indianapolis for this training on a regular basis. The result was that retailers utilizing association services had the most modern-looking stores in the towns and cities in which they operated.

WHOLESALE LEADERS

There are probably dozens of outstanding wholesale executives who could (and maybe should) be profiled, but this book will focus on just a few.

Richard (Dick) Hesse

Dick Hesse was one of 5 retailers from Chicago who formed their own wholesale company back in the 1920s. It was not a dealer-owned firm; it was privately owned by the 5 men. Dick closed his store and became the CEO (though that term wasn't used way back when) of the new firm, called Ace Hardware.

So retailers buying from it could compete with chain competition, Ace established some different margins—2% adder on any merchandise bought and shipped directly from a manufacturer; 6% adder on any merchandise "pooled"—that is, group orders placed and merchandise received and shipped directly to ordering retailers without being put on the wholesaler's shelves, and 9% on merchandise shipped from the wholesaler's warehouse. He pioneered those margins. Dealer-owned firms at the time did not operate with such low margins—firms like American Hardware Supply out of Pittsburgh or Our Own Hardware out of Minneapolis.

Hesse built Ace into one of the industry's largest distribution firms, expanding it beyond Chicago as the years passed. Upon his death, as pre-arranged, the company became a dealer-owned company. Today it is the world's largest hardware wholesale firm and operates in more than 60 countries around the world as well as in all 50 states. Thousands of retailers here in the U. S. and elsewhere are identified as Ace Hardware.

Interestingly, Ace Hardware stores have been recognized for the past several years as providing the "best service of any retailer", even though the company is not a chain but consists of more than 4,000 individually owned outlets.

John Cotter

John Cotter did not invent dealer-owned wholesaling, but the charismatic Cotter built his company founded in 1948 into what was, for a time, the largest dealer-owned wholesaler in the world, even though he didn't begin his company until the postwar period, whereas others preceded him for decades.

John Cotter was a promoter and a merchant par excellent. With his longtime associate, Ed Lanctot, he put together national advertising and got his dealers to distribute millions of direct mail pieces. When he learned that the True Value name, originally owned by a bankrupt Hibbard, Spencer, Bartlett & Co. of nearby Evanston, Illinois, would be available, he bought it. The name, he felt, was far better than the V & S (standing for Value & Service) private brand and store identity name he was using for products and as a store name.

Retailers began adopting the True Value name, and the company's heavy advertising program helped make it one of the best known brand names in the hardware industry. The company later changed its corporate name to True Value Hardware.

Over the years, Cotter also acquired a number of other, smaller dealer-owned firms, among them Great Western Hardware and Southwest Hardware of California and Walter H. Allen Co. of Texas. He also recruited top executives from wholesalers who were closing up shop and they served as super recruiters of new member dealers and in other key executive positions within the company.

Arnold Gerberding and Don Wolf

Two other men who were very influential in the postwar industry were Arnold Gerberding, who founded Hardware Wholesalers, Inc., at the end of the war, and Don Wolf, who succeeded him and built the company into a billion-dollar wholesaler, before turning the company over to Mike McClelland. The company is now headed by Bob Taylor, a former retail member who had served on the board and as chairman of the board. The company's name changed to Do it Best Corp. It had begun using Do it Best as the name of its store identify program.

Gerberding's vision of dealer-ownership was different from that of other dealer-owned firms at the time. Gerberding felt that Hardware Wholesalers should serve both lumber/building material dealers as well as hardware stores, and right from the beginning, its merchandise offerings included lumber and building materials, merchandise simply not offered by any other dealer-owned for many years.

When Don Wolf took over, the company was doing $30+ million in sales and was not yet a national company. Under his leadership, it grew sales to more than $1 billion, expanded its territory and opened additional distribution centers. Today it is the second largest dealer-owned firm in America and the world.

Wolf retired at 64 and was succeeded by Mike McClelland, who led the company and oversaw its continued growth. Under McClelland, the company merged with Our Own Hardware,one of the pioneer dealer-owned and he, upon his retirement, was succeeded by Bob Taylor, who had been a board member and chairman of the company before taking over as CEO. Taylor's family operates several Do it Best stores in Virginia Beach, Virginia.

Dealer-owned pioneers

Dealer-owned wholesalers have existed in the hardware industry for many years. Some have succeeded greatly, others failed or did not grow to a sufficient size as to be competitive and were bought out or closed.

Among the many managers of some of the early dealer-owned firms were men like William (Bill) Stout, Le Herron, John Berryman and Larry Zehfuss of American Hardware Supply Co., of Pittsburgh and later, Butler, Pennsylvania. The firm later changed its name to ServiStar,its store identity name and ultimately merged with Cotter & Co. to become True Value Hardware.

Another pioneer dealer-owned was Our Own Hardware of Minneapolis, headed for years by Steve Duffy and later by Hank Parsinen and Hugh Byrne.

Other wholesalers who made a difference

William George (Bill) Steltz, Sr., president of Supplee-Biddle-Steltz Co., a wholesaler that was based in Philadelphia and which has been out of business for years, was the founder of a wholesale group known as Liberty Distributors, comprised of non-competitive wholesale executives who met periodically to exchange information. It was formed during the latter years of the Depression.

Later, the firm began some group buying, developed some private brands and produced direct mail circulars and catalogs for members to offer retail customers. Among its brand names was Trustworthy, which continues to exist and is being used by some retailers as a store name. Steltz also developed a special toy catalog that was offered to other wholesalers selling toys. It was called Billy & Ruth, named for his two children, one of which, Bill Steltz, Jr., later succeeded him as head of the Philadelphia distributorship.

Paul Cosgrave, who had been with a Minneapolis wholesale firm, founded another wholesale group, Pro Hardware, which provides products, store identity and promotional material through member wholesalers to retailers. Pro Hardware stores continue to exist, as does the Pro headquarters organization, which now also serves specialty distributors and retailers. Harold Dungan succeeded Cosgrave and was its head for many years. Gary Cosgrave, Paul's son, is now chairman of the organization.

Still another wholesale group was formed in the postwar period, this one headquartered in Cleveland, Ohio, and organized by Norman Luekens, president of The George Worthington, Co. Called Sentry Hardware, it was managed first by Clifford Palmquist, formerly with the Farwell, Ozmun, Kirk & Co. of St. Paul, Minnesota, and later by Richard Brant, who began his career with Hibbard, Spencer, Bartlett & Co., then spent time with Morley Bros. of Saginaw, Michigan, and with the National Retail Hardware Association.

Today, Distribution America is the result of a merger between surviving wholesalers who belonged to Liberty Distributors and Sentry Hardware.

One individual wholesaler who certainly deserves mention is Joe Orgill, whose privately-owned company based in Memphis, Tennessee, is today the world's largest privately owned hardware distributor. The Orgill firm, now headed by Ron Beal and before that by Bill Fondren, generates more than $1 billion in sales and now operates throughout the United States and in a number of foreign countries. It was one of the early converts to one-story distribution centers and computerization and now operates multiple, very efficient centers around the country to service its retail customers.

ASSOCIATION EXECUTIVES

William P. (Bill) Farrell

Bill Farrell was the second full-time executive of the American Hardware Manufacturers Association after it moved to Chicago and built that association into a major industry force and influence. He began his hardware career as a journalist in 1957, first with *Hardware Age* magazine and later as editor of *Hardware Merchandiser* magazine. AHMA's first full-time executive was Sam Mitchell, but he served in that capacity only a few years, before being succeeded by Farrell.

Farrell was responsible for the expansion of AHMA's activities into all of the services outlined in the chapter profiling industry associations (Chapter 8). Among other accomplishments, he developed the industry's first electronic order-entry system, helped manufacturers increase export sales via international trade show pavilions and catalogs and developed educational efforts with Thunderbird University as well as a technology conference, now called the Hardlines Technology Forum™ which brings together members of all 3 distribution levels. He retired as CEO several years ago but remains active with the association as vice chairman of the board. His son, Tim, succeeded him as CEO.

Dozens, maybe hundreds of other association executives played leading roles in helping members of the industry survive and prosper during the competitive postwar period. Too many to profile all of them, but some of the others certainly deserve mention.

William G. (Bill) Mashaw

When Russ Mueller died, NRHA's board named William G. (Bill) Mashaw to succeed him, and Mashaw continued the fine work Mueller had started. He was Managing Director of NRHA for many years, helped it further expand its Research Department, oversaw the continued development of the magazine, including its name change to *Do It Yourself Retailing,* and NRHA's move into a new, larger headquarters building. When he retired, he was succeeded by another longtime NRHA executive, Rick Lambert, who had headed NRHA's Industry Activities department for decades, responsible for developing and selling industry-wide promotions.

John Hammond

Hammond, who retired in 2008 after being with NRHA for 38 years, began as an associate editor and became editor of its magazine before being named Managing Director in 1994. NRHA had by then suffered a series of financial setbacks and had depleted many of its reserves, accumulated over decades.

He nursed the association back to health, developed new publishing ventures to bring in income, oversaw the development of direct memberships and signing up of retailers affiliated with wholesalers as members, incorporated Canadian retailers into its membership so it could become the North American Retail Hardware Association, retiring after his 14-year tenure with the organization once again a solid, highly respected entity in the industry.

Other noteworthy individuals

Bernie Marcus and Arthur Blank—these two men founded The Home Depot and changed retailing of all kinds with their warehouse format. Their 3rd partner, Pat Farrah, did not remain with the company as it grew to dominate the home center industry. Home Depot, with its bare-bones look, low prices and heavy advertising, plus stacks and stacks of merchandise, encouraged other retailers around the world to copy its format. It also led to the demise of many of the pioneer home center chains.

Robert (Bob) Tillman— the one-time store manager who, as CEO of Lowe's, transformed the company and grew it into the second largest home center chain in the world. He moved from small town America to the nation's largest cities, from primarily operating in the south into a national chain. He modified the warehouse format of Home Depot, upgraded it and moved the company into metro areas, where previously it had focused on smaller cities mostly in the south and midwest.

Charles Snitow—as previously profiled in this book, Snitow created the National Hardware Show® in 1946 and built it into a mammoth, industry-wide event, providing a showcase for thousands of manufacturers to introduce their products to the world over its decades of existence.

Lee Waterman—he introduced Corningware to the world, a revolutionary new cookware, and became very active in industry associations. He headed Corning's consumer product division for many years and helped the hardware and housewares industry reap tremendous sales from Pyrex and Corningware, both products being mainstays of housewares departments in postwar hardware stores. He was so successful that he also later served as the company's president for a number of years.

Frank Lucier—while there are many men who have been affiliated with Black & Decker in the postwar period, as CEO of the nation's largest power tool firm Lucier was the one who managed it during the period of its greatest growth, helping it develop a wider variety of products than just drills.

Jack Bates—was the industry executive from The Stanley Works who was most active in the industry, serving as president of AHMA, and working closely with NRHA on industry programs and services and who was truly dedicated to all levels of distribution in the hardware industry.

Norris Aldeen—another longtime industry leader, he was president of Amerock Corp. for many years and provided leadership not only in store merchandising systems but in association matters as well.

Two other individuals deserving mention are both retailers.

Tom Chasteen, a retailer in Florida, brought together a small group of retailers more than two decades ago for an idea-exchange conference. It has grown over the years into a very important and significant gathering of independent hardware, home center and lumber/building material dealers, attracting hundreds annually and now supported by many of the country's leading wholesalers. Some 40-50 manufacturers' executives attend to interact with retailers firsthand. Wholesalers now support the meetings, too. Each year proceeds from various fund-raising programs during the meeting are donated to charities, in excess of $20,000 annually in recent years. Beginning in 2010, at the suggestion of attending retailers, a number of wholesale buyers will be honored in recognition of their difficult job in satisfying hundreds or thousands of retailers buying from their respective firms.

John Fix III, a retailer from Eastchester, a city north of Manhattan, operates *Hardlines,* a blog that reaches several thousand retailers around the country daily, who find it a great place to share ideas and get answers to problems about their computer systems, find sources of supply for hard-to-find items, identify promising new merchandise categories to add to inventory. . . or simply to exchange best wishes with each other.

Among the many other individuals who deserve mention, at least, are some identified by *Home Channel News*, an industry publication, in a list compiled in 1999. Here are some (not all) of those people, mostly pioneer home center retailers and a few wholesalers, plus others who have had a major influence in the industry since 1999.

Harold and Mel Cohen, Brothers who created Somerville Lumber, one of the highest volume independent dealers this industry had ever seen at the time

Stanley Cohen, ran Central Hardware, an institution in St. Louis, for decades.

Jim Cohen, Stanley's son and Central Hardware president, who presided over its sale to Handy Andy in 1989. Central filed Chapter 11 in 1993.

Ray Cooney, former Scotty's president, big advocate for centralized warehousing. Became a consultant for Alcoa's retail interests in South America.

Dan Cotter, Cotter & Co. president, son of John, who engineered merger with ServiStar, one of the pioneer dealer-owned wholesalers.

Norm Darrer, President of Moore's until its acquisition by Hope Lumber in 1997. Also stepped in and tried to save Mr. HOW Warehouse for Service Merchandise. All now gone.

Chuck Davis, President of Rickel, one of the pioneer home centers, in the early '80s, when the retailer was owned by Supermarkets General (SGC). Helped engineer management-led leveraged buyout of SGC, whose debt crippled Rickel's operations.

Alonzo G. Decker Jr. His father, Alonzo G. Decker Sr., co-founded Black & Decker (with Duncan Black) in 1910. Alonzo Jr. started working for the company in 1930, became president in 1960 and retired in 1979 at the age of 70.

Frank Denny, Former president of W.R. Grace home center division, who founded Builders Square, later acquired by Kmart and now gone.

Richard England, Longtime chairman of Washington, DC's Hechinger, dubbed the "World's Most Unusual Lumberyard." One of the pioneer home center chains.

Fred Erb, Built Erb Lumber, which began in 1922, into a 47-unit operation, before selling to Carolina Holdings in July 1993 for $77.5 million. Also helped develop what became DIY Home Warehouse in Cleveland. All gone now.

Steve Erlbaum, Driving force behind Mr. Goodbuys, one of the more stylish warehouse home centers ever — if only it could have been profitable.

Pat Farrah, Home Depot's flamboyant heart, soul and merchandising guru. One of its 3 founders who left early, then returned later for a while.

Dan Ferguson, Former Newell chairman, who set a standard for buying companies making staple products and focusing on keeping retailers in stock.

Leonard Gertler, second-generation head of family-owned All American Home Center, for years a mecca for industry executives that endures in L.A.-area market.

J. Peter Grace, Patriarch of W.R. Grace, which in the 1970s acquired home center chains whose combined sales were the highest in the industry in the early 1980s.

Mike Grossman, Longtime president of Grossman's, a family business that dated back to 1894, and which rose to become the leading lumberyard retailer in New England through the 1970s. Before Home Depot.

Herbert Haimsohn, Chairman of Handyman, one of the first true home center operators in California. Handyman grew to 88 stores, but its parent, Edison Brothers, liquidated its properties to cash in on the state's real estate boom.

George Hanzi, One of the industry's genuine innovators. Helped found Handy City and later developed Homecrafters Warehouse. When these ventures were sold or went bust, Hanzi started an upscale hardlines store called Charleston Forge which — given the popularity of Restoration Hardware today — was ahead of its time.

Joe Hardy, Founder and chairman of 84 Lumber, who built his company into the largest privately owned lumberyard chain in America. Business is now run by his daughter.

John Hechinger Sr., Longtime CEO of Hechinger, a company his father, Sidney, started in 1919. Hechinger firm became a nonpareil merchant in the 1970s—before Home Depot, with Phil Mansfield the merchandising guru.

David Heerensperger, Chairman of Pay 'N Pak, who sold his business and used the proceeds to create Eagle Hardware & Garden, one of the few warehouse dealers that stood his ground against Home Depot. Later bought by Lowe's

Jim Inglis, Former Handyman and Dixieline Lumber exec, who rose to power at Home Depot, led the development of Expo Design Centers and stressed international growth.

Maynard Jenkins, Former chairman of Orchard Supply Hardware, who expanded chain into southern California and took company public. Orchard's success proved hardware stores could coexist with warehouse competition. Now owned by Sears.

Harvey Knell, President of Ole's, the Rosemead, Calif.-based home center chain founded by his father, Max, that Knell grew to 35 outlets before selling it to W.R.Grace in 1986. Ole's is now gone.

Ed Lanctot, For decades, Cotter & Co.'s lead merchant.

Mike and Brian McCoy, Co-presidents of McCoy's Building Supply Centers in Texas, one of the industry's largest regional retailers, which was started by their father, Emmett.

John Menard, Took a pole barn operation in Eau Claire, Wis., in 1960 and grew it into Menards, the industry's third-largest dealer and largest private company. Menard is an avid race car aficionado.

John Parsons vp-home improvement at Sears in the 1980s. Helped develop the first Sears Paint and Hardware stores, which eventually became Sears Hardware.

Robert Pergament, Marketing whiz to brother Murray's financial and real estate acumen at Pergament Home Centers, for years a prominent chain in New York metro area.

Alan Petersen, American Tools, built a midwestern maker of Vise Grip hand tools into an international giant by acquiring other companies, before selling out.

Dale Pond, Ex-Payless Cashways, HQ Warehouse and Montgomery Ward exec, who became Lowe's chief merchant. Named one of nation's top 100 marketing executives by a major business magazine.

George Poulos, The definition of industry veteran, whose resume includes stints at Wolohan Lumber and Lampert Lumber, and who got his second wind as a turnaround specialist at Diamond Lumber, Robertson Cos. and, finally, at Leeds Building Products.

Ron Rashkow, Owner of Chicago-area Handy Andy Home Improvement centers, which he built into a $700 million business, but saw it get caught in the Menard-Home Depot-Builders Square shootout in his markets.

Al Rickel, Co-founded Rickel Home Centers with brother Bob in 1948. One of first true home centers with an indoor lumber department.

Harvey Rosen, Handyman's president in the 1980s, who presided over the liquidation of that once-dominant retailer.

Sanford Sigoloff, Turnaround specialist dubbed Ming the Merciless. Notoriously remembered for firing Bernie Marcus and Arthur Blank from Daylin.

David Stanley, Former president of Payless Cashways, whose aggressive acquisitions in the 1980s grew Payless into a nationwide entity. Stanley joined

Payless from Minneapolis firm Piper Jaffray Hopwood and his presence augured the growing importance of investors and bankers in the industry. Was forced to take Payless private — and assume nearly $1 billion in debt — to block a hostile takeover bid, a move that, in retrospect, buried the company.

Jim Stewart, Lone Star Industries chief, who in the '60s and '70s acquired regional dealers to develop national chain. Retail division was was sold off piecemeal in 1978.

Bob Strickland, Lowe's legendary chairman was a major spokesman for "home improvement retailing" to Wall Street and spearheaded industry-wide research initiatives.

Jim Sweet, Scotty's founder and one of the best-liked people in the industry until he left the chain in 1988. Engineered selling a piece of Scotty's to Belgium's GB-Inno-BM, for $10 million. .

John Walker, Flamboyant Lowe's executive and "super salesman" during company's early pro-oriented years. At one trade show brought what he said was $1 million in cash onto the stage with him as a prop.

Charles West, Chairman of West Building Materials, one of the industry's strongest pro yards at one time. West once operated 67 units.

Richard Wolohan, Wolohan Lumber, a principal in the early days of Wickes before starting his own company, thus gave birth to two chains.

Larry Zehfuss, President of ServiStar under whose watch it expanded its market reach.

Mike McClelland, CEO of Do it Best Corp. for many years, having taken over from Don Wolf. Now affiliated with the BIG Group of independent hardware and home center chains.

Bob Taylor, current CEO of Do it Best Corp., whose family operates DIB stores in Virginia and who had been a board member and past chairman of the dealer-owned firm.

And to the hundreds of other industry veterans and leaders who helped shape and grow the industry in the postwar years but who are not mentioned in this book, we extend our apologies.

Chapter Twelve

SIGNIFICANT EVENTS OF THE POSTWAR PERIOD

In the 60-plus years since the end of World War II, the hardware industry has faced many challenges—both internally and from exterior forces. Who is to say which was the worst—or the best?

Without doubt, the development of computers is one of the most important positive influences, making possible the expansion and growth of retailers, wholesalers and manufacturers in the industry. Their development, ever-lower pricing and ever-greater capabilities are largely responsible today for multi-billion dollar wholesalers, more efficient warehouses (at all levels of distribution) and improved return-on-investment for retailers stocking tens of thousands of products.

Without computers, the sheer volume of data generated by multi-million and multi-billion dollar retailers and wholesalers would be completely overwhelming to this—or any—industry.

Technical developments in computerization continue to be mind-boggling, with smart phones today having, probably, more capacity than the early, huge computers put to work in hardware wholesale firms.   Today retailers can check their systems and find out how many individual items they sold yesterday, last week, last month or last year.   When they plan a trip to their major wholesaler's buying market, they can come to the show knowing exactly what they bought, what they sold and what they have left over from that sure-fire new item they discovered there last year.

While computers point out bad buys, they also free up capital at both wholesaling and retailing by limiting those buying mistakes and help merchants concentrate more of their investment dollars on the best sellers, which enables both channels to experiment and add new lines and categories. And at the retail level, it is this willingness to try something new that continues to keep independent retailing alive and in competition with the giants of the industry.

Probably the other most significant event—negative for the hardware trade—was the emergence of discounters, or as they are now known, mass merchandisers. Mass merchandisers have affected every retail field. They sell everything that was available in the many family-owned businesses to be found on America's Main Streets and have decimated Main Streets across America. The toll also turned out to be very severe on mass merchandisers themselves. In the early stages of their development, there were dozens, maybe as many as a hundred, discount firms started by retail entrepreneurs.

Firms like Bradlees, Calgor, E J Korvette, Masters, Ayr-way, Woolco and dozens of others disappeared as better managed, more disciplined retailers like Walmart and Target expanded and then encroached on their trading areas. Low prices could attract consumers but smart management skills were needed to survive.

Chain stores also grew at an amazing pace in the postwar decades, and emerged and became more dominating in fields previously largely unaffected by them. Consolidation is continuing in that field, as it did in mass merchandising. Take the drug store field as an example. Today two chains dominate that channel of distribution—Walgreens and CVS Caremark, whereas there used to be more than a dozen quite successful regional or local drug store chains. A third, Rite Aid, still operates but is nowhere near as successful as the other two. CVS in particular has been busy acquiring regional chains such as its recent take-over of Longs Drugs on the West Coast. Independent drug stores on the Main Streets of America, or in its shopping centers, are hard to find, but you'll likely find Walgreen and CVS drug stores facing each other across many busy intersections.

Indeed, shopping centers also changed the face—and location—of all kinds of retailing in the postwar period. The first shopping center is generally said to have been built in Framingham, Massachusetts. It was soon copied elsewhere and department stores became anchor units, especially when enclosed malls came into being, helping bring customers to these huge, multi-store retail emporiums. Sears became an anchor in hundreds of shopping malls, but began departing from some in 2008 and 2009 as its lustre dimmed.

Not every retailer—and certainly not hardware stores— could afford the rent in an air conditioned, heated mall, so strip shopping centers began attracting merchants like hardware retailers and independent home centers. The retail scene changed again when giant home centers (and other big-boxes) appeared—big enough to stand alone and powerful enough to attract consumers on their own, without needing the appeal of other types of retail outlets.

These location options lead to the development of more specialty chains, firms like Bed, Bath & Beyond in the housewares field; Office Depot and Office Max replacing the local office supply retailer, and Best Buy or strong regional chains like H. H. Gregg replacing the local appliance dealer. Now some of these non-competitive big-box retailers sit side by side in mega big-box shopping centers.

Of course, as previously noted, nothing affected the hardware industry more than the development and ultimate domination of the industry by The Home Depot and Lowe's. Those two firms forced most pioneer home center chains out of business. They could not compete on price; they could not compete on systems or promotions; their locations became outdated. Whatever could go wrong seemed to go wrong. Only privately-owned Menards, operating in the Midwest, seems to have been able to grow when competing directly with one or both of the giants.

Elsewhere, there are individual stores or local chains who are surviving—firms like All American Home Center of Downey, California, with a Home Depot now facing the firm across a parking lot, or Jerry's Home Centers in Oregon or hardware chains like Westlake Ace, W. E. Aubuchon Co., and others or lumber/building material chains like Foxworth-Galbraith, headquartered in Dallas, Texas.

Yes, there are thousands of individual survivors across America even as other kinds of retailers try to cherry-pick some of the basic items on which the hardware industry has relied for decades. Today's supermarket

An example of the attractive retail sales floors the American consumer finds today in thousands of independently owned or small chain hardware stores, lumberyards or home centers.

is offering a handful of small hand tools, light bulbs and electric sundries, maybe a few plumbing items, some hardware items like padlocks, packets of nails, screws, etc. You'll also find lower priced housewares items and, in season, toys.

Drug store chains like Walgreens and CVS Caremark and your neighborhood convenience store/gas station also are stocking many of these items, offering the American consumer plenty of "convenient" choices for his or her hardware purchases.

The great unknown for the future is, of course, the Internet. How much will American consumers rely on the Internet for their purchases? Will they turn to it for their everyday, smaller-cost items or will they rely mostly on it for their unusual and/or big-ticket items where savings might be quite substantial?

Retailers of all kinds, including hardware and lumber/building material retailers, now have their own web sites. Hardware wholesalers sometimes use their web sites to make consumer sales for their affiliated retailers, in some cases encouraging consumers to pick up their purchases at a local store. Such efforts serve to introduce those stores to consumers and hopefully make them regular shoppers in the future.

There is no doubt web retailing will continue to grow, but how much it will affect the hardware industry is still something of an unknown.

But none of the big chain stores mentioned earlier, not even home center giants like The Home Depot and Lowe's, offers quite the merchandise range or multiple brands of many privately owned or small chain hardware stores, home centers or lumber/building material dealers.

And these surviving retailers keep developing new lines and categories—telephones, pet supplies, metal detectors, water gardening. The list is amazing and almost endless.

Go to any wholesaler's buying market or trade show today and you'll see dozens, maybe hundreds, of new-to-market vendors offering hundreds or maybe thousands of new items. Some will fail, but others will bring excitement and sales to retailers stocking them. And more reasons for the American consumer to continue shopping in a hardware store, home center or lumber/building material dealer near them.

One with interesting new items. . . one with a good location. . . one with experienced, helpful employees. . . one which satisfies their needs.

ChapterThirteen

What's ahead?

What will the future hold for the hardware industry?

The only thing on which there is likely to be agreement is: continuing competition.

The industry is going to require greater professionalism at all levels. Independent retailers will need to continue differentiating themselves from their chain store and larger competitors, while also being better managers of their own businesses. This means being better at budgeting, employee training, long range planning, and being sure that the people they employ can perform as jobs demand.

Women will continue to be of growing importance in the industry— to be courted as customers, to be sought as employees and to be recognized as store owners. So will the Hispanic population be of growing importance, especially as customers and employees.

Whereas the American consumer shifted some years ago from Do It Yourself to Do It For Me, he and she will continue shifting back to DIY for some time. Given current economic conditions, consumers will be focusing more on smaller projects, not massive remodelings or expensive projects. This means the industry will have to learn to live with flatter sales growth.

Competition will continue to include the two home center giants and, in the Midwest, Menards, though it seems likely that the new-store count among the two publicly-owned chains will be down from previous years. Too many big-city markets are now fully stored and in many cases, over-stored. This cutback in store openings occurred in 2009 and will continue for a few years into the future.

Farm supply chains like Tractor Supply are growing at a solid rate and will be expanding into new markets, too. Better-managed chains catering to lower income consumers, like Family Dollar and Dollar General, will peck away at some categories basic to the hardware industry, while Walmart will continue to be a major competitor for the lawn and garden category, for light bulbs and in some stores, for paint. It certainly will continue to be a significant factor in the housewares market, but will remain weak in tools, plumbing and anything electrical except its massive assortment of light bulbs. Target will be a housewares competitor but of negligible concern for basic lines. Kmart is turning out to be less of a problem than it used to be, even with the addition of Sears brands to its inventories.

Supermarkets are not likely to give up their seasonal efforts behind some lawn and garden and outdoor living categories, Christmas decorations and will continue stocking lower end housewares, some tools and little fix-up items. They will continue to be a convenience outlet, not a destination competitor.

As this book was being written in the latter months of 2009, independent retailers were coping with reduced sales volume, sometimes of as much as 20% and 30%, and exchanging ideas via John Fix's *Hardlines* blog on what they were doing to survive. Their ingenuity was keeping them as survivors as they cut expenses, sought out niches to attract sales and found new ways to be of service to commercial and consumer customers in their trading areas.

Many learned of research showing that 70% of consumers admitted that end cap displays were very effective in capturing their attention in stores and that they were paying more attention to departmental signs in order to improve their shopping experiences. So frequently changing displays and signing them properly was becoming an operational necessity for everyone as 2009 was winding down.

In addition to trying to identify unmet needs in the local marketplace and establishing new niche departments, retailers also are realizing that they can become destinations for specific products by having the best and broadest selection of some basic items—such as specialty light bulbs. . . or cookie cutters. . . or vacuum bags, belts and filters. . . and surrounding their checkstands with unique, impulse-generating products that appeal to both male and female customers.

Bridal registries long have been offered by retailers strong in housewares. One retailer now is establishing a by-mail "wish list" for males to spur sales of his sporting goods, tools and other male-oriented departments—and is spreading the word of this effort to other retailers. Ingenuity like this is another way of coping and being a leader as one way of surviving into the future.

Perhaps the most pressing need continues to be finding a way for the "average" retailer to improve stockturns. Even with computers now providing item-sales records, too many retailers are still not achieving 4 stockturns a year on their inventory. Some retailers manage it while still carrying all those hard-to-find items which give them a competitive advantage in the marketplace, but too many do not.

Wholesalers and manufacturers have done much to improve supply chain efficiencies, achieved partly because computers made such efficiencies possible, but more needs to be done, especially in order for retailers to be the "destination retailer" for more products for more customers.

Recognizing the need for youthful talent

One of the strengths of the independent hardware industry over the years has been the "family" aspect. Many hardware stores and lumberyards have been owned and managed by several generations, some for 100 years or more.

Unfortunately, as stated elsewhere in this book, during the 70s and 80s, some members of the younger retailing generations saw more opportunities in other fields, without the concerns and competition that faced them in continuing a family-run business.

The National Retail Hardware Association recognized that fact decades ago, as did its publication, *Hardware Retailing*, with special sections such as "Perpetuating the Family Business" and hardbound books encouraging these newer generations to continue a career in the retailing business.

In 1996, John Hammond, NRHA's Managing Director, came up with a new program aimed more specifically at encouraging the next generation to make hardware retailing their career. It's called the "Young Retailer of the Year" program.

It honors outstanding (35 and under) individuals in the industry for their achievements and demonstrates why making the retail business a career has many rewards. Nominees for the award can be retail store employees or members of the owner's family. The submissions come from industry wholesalers, store owners, the individuals themselves or other interested parties who've spotted these outstanding young men and women.

Individuals are nominated in one of three categories—businesses under $2 million in sales; over $2 million and multiple store operations. A presentation is submitted which describes the person's achievements. It is focused on personal achievements, not the store's overall success, although the two do go hand-in-hand.

The first awards program was held in Chicago in 1997, with distributors, retailers and other industry representatives attending. After that initial year, the awards program became part of the annual NRHA convention and has become one of the highlights of the meeting.

A video of the person's achievements is produced and shown to the banquet audience and has proven to be an inspiration to many others. The videos are posted on the NRHA web site for anyone in the industry to view.

Over the 13 years of the program's existence, 92 individuals have been honored and hundreds have been nominated for this honor, a convincing demonstration that the "next generation" of hardware and lumber/building material retailers is indeed alive, well and ready to tackle the opportunities and challenges of the future.

Honorees have ranged from a teenage employee headed for college who decided to purchase the store he worked in from the aging owners, and who has built it into a multi-store success, to dozens of sons and daughters who have taken their family businesses to new heights.

The program is supported by the American Hardware Manufacturers Association and three major manufacturers—3M Co., which was the original sponsor, plus Cooper Tools and Scotts Miracle Gro.

Hammond, who retired in 2008 after 14 years as Managing Director of the North American Retail Hardware Association, believes the industry faces another severe challenge in the future. "In addition to attracting a new breed of younger store owners, independent hardware stores and home centers face a real challenge in attracting the new, young generation of customers. While attracting more women is also an important issue, I believe this age or generation problem may be even bigger in the long run.

"The hardware stores' most loyal customers are 'seniors'. Young people today are predisposed to shop large format retailers, having grown up with these merchants. The baby boomers who shop hardware stores will buy less and less over the next couple of decades and merchants need to attract these younger customers with smart new marketing and a savvy and satisfying in-store shopping experiences. Too many don't do so well at the present with this class of customer."

There are challenges facing the industry's manufacturers and wholesalers as well as the industry looks ahead.

Just as this book was being finalized, the North American Retail Hardware Association and *Hardware Retailing* magazine conducted a webinar (web-based seminar) called, "The future of home improvement retailing." Some of the predictions made were based on extensive surveys conducted among more than 100 retailers, wholesale executives and manufacturing executives.

What did these execs and NRHA think and predict? NRHA predicts a 2.4% compound annual growth for the next 5 years for the hardware industry, for one thing. The industry panel was a bit more confident, estimating compound annual growth will be 3.2% for the next 5 years. Both smaller than that enjoyed during the decade before, but still indicating a growing market.

The consensus was that maintenance and repair products and projects will be the growth drivers of the next several years, not big, expensive projects.

The industry panel predicted that tomorrow's consumer will be increasingly focused on the price and quality of products. They will be demanding better service, selection and information. Providing those while coping with margin pressures will be the challenge facing the industry's retailers.

Retailers among the research panel felt these would be major customer demands more than did the wholesalers and manufacturers participating in the research.

It thus seems quite obvious that hardware and lumber/building material retailers need to continue discovering niches—items and categories that fit the needs (or wants) of consumers in their area, things not available from other nearby competitive retailers, which will drive traffic into their stores and allow customers to realize that these stores and their employees offer them interesting products as well as being able to help solve everyday DIY needs.

Industry manufacturers will need to help retailers develop those unique and sales-generating niches, as will full line and specialty distributors.

Many independent retailers are doing an excellent job in identifying niche opportunities; it will continue to be a necessity.

There will be a need for retailers to provide more installation services, admittedly a difficult aspect of retailing, but with unemployment higher than it has been, the talent pool of people who could provide such services for retailers is greater than ever, so maybe the opportunity can be realized.

Retailers will need to continue upgrading their stores, using power aisles, dump bins, end caps and creative merchandise presentations, just as the survivors have been doing these past few decades.

A major future problem

It was probably 30 or more years ago that NRHA and *Hardware Retailing* focused the industry's attention on a major problem, that of business perpetuation, one that hasn't entirely gone away as the years have gone by. Today the problem is even greater than it was long ago, since so many successful retailers are now generating far greater sales and have accrued such a large investment that finding men and women with the funds to buy out these successful businesses is going to be doubly hard if there is no one in the immediate families with the desire to take over the business.

NRHA's Young Retailer program is an important step in the right direction, but more will need to be done to perpetuate stores.

It is a problem program wholesalers need to address much more aggressively than they have to date. They must find ways to help new owners acquire these larger-than-ever retail outlets. It is a problem NRHA also needs to consider in all its ramifications and develop some guidelines to help current owners ready their businesses for continuation, as well as to guide prospective buyers to make wise decisions.

The trade association's future role?

The industry's major trade associations also need to evaluate their current, existing programs to see what else might be needed to insure the industry's continuation.

Throughout its history, the retailers' association, NRHA, has evolved to meeting the changing needs of the nation's independent hardware stores, home centers and lumberyards. The programs and services that NRHA offers independent retailers today are quite different from those in the past and reflect the dramatic changes in the channel since the 1980's and need to be different.

While in the past NRHA offered the industry diverse services such as store planning and design and national consumer advertising programs, today it is focused on helping members become better, more profitable retailers through an array of information, training and communications.

For the first time in its history, in 2010 NRHA will become a true national trade organization, directly serving all retailers throughout the United States and Canada. More than ever, NRHA says, the independent retailer today needs to execute at a more sophisticated level in order to succeed— to pursue excellence in store operations, and the association says it will continue to use new technologies in reaching out to the next generation of young retailers who respond to new ways of communicating, including electronic newsletters, webinars, social networking, online videos and web-based training programs.

According to NRHA's Managing Director, Bill Lee, "All channel partners must work together to ensure the future of independent retailers; it is good for everyone – retailers, manufacturers and wholesalers alike." Its Vendor Partner program allows manufacturers to work together with NRHA to provide product information and product knowledge training to retailers and helps manufacturers better understand the independent market.

According to the American Hardware Manufacturers Association as this book was going to the publisher in the final months of 2009, there was too much uncertainty in the short-term economic/political arena to make quick and likely unneeded additions to existing programs, services and activities, many of which were discussed in the chapter on associations describing AHMA's role in the industry. This uncertainty has created a significant amount of "restraint" upon manufacturers, and therefore AHMA, until there is a much clearer and defined road map for the future.

Long term, when the landscape clears, AHMA says it will continue its 108 years-old tradition of serving the manufacturing segment of the industry specifically, and in a broader sense the entire industry, with the needed and required array of programs, services and activities as indicated by its members and industry trends, and as directed and approved by the association's Board of Directors.

Once known only for its annual trade show, today's International Housewares Association (IHA) is developing new services and activities for the benefit of hardware and home center retailers selling housewares products, as well as for its nearly 1,600 members. Its show continues to be important as a source of new items and new ideas. Hardware and home center retailers are able to get new merchandising ideas by checking photos of winners of IHA's *Global Innovator* program, honoring retailers around the world for their housewares merchandising prowess.

IHA now is providing year-round education and industry information through its annual State of the Industry Report; quarterly *Housewares MarketWatch* with consumer panel and retail tracking data from NPD; and specialty retailer education, both at the Show and on its website. *MarketWatch* provides suppliers with information to help retailers better understand consumer sentiment.

Recognizing that there is a dearth of market data for housewares suppliers to use with their retail partners in strategic planning, IHA began a new research initiative in 2009 that seeks to provide credible volume estimates for major housewares categories. Going forward, IHA will include categories of interest to hardware retailers, including storage and cleaning products and small electrics for kitchen, personal care and household.

One retailer's future thoughts

Probably no one offers a better outline of what independent retailers need to consider and do for a profitable, growing future than Alan Talman, owner of Karp's Hardware on Long Island, who sent a list of his ideas to the several thousand retailers who participate in *Hardlines,* the blog originated by retailer John Fix III of New York state.   Here are Talman's observations:

What should/could/would I do to get more business out of this town or trading area?

"This is the most important question any one of us can ask. It's universal—small store or large; it's the ONE question. We are wrong if we expect the customer to search us out. We have to go get them.

Here's a checklist that I've been working on for a while. This assumes that you're already doing the stuff the co-ops or your primary wholesaler urge you to do— like good product mix and realistic pricing. Here are the questions all of us should ask ourselves.

1. Are you well represented on the web? You would not open in a business in 1980 without being in the Yellow Pages. This is not 1980 anymore. The web doesn't have to cost money. You can do it for nearly zero investment.

2. Do you diversify your customer base? Do you have some contacts with local restaurants, factories, schools, the Boy Scouts, handymen from Church, landscapers, contractors, masons, etc? If not, why not? Visit job sites, bring donuts. Make up flyers for contractors. Press your church to set up an account for its handyman. Tell your plumbers that you're open on Sunday, you know their plumbing supply house isn't. Dry cleaners buy a lot of V-Belts. Body shops buy bolts. The local garbage dump might become your best customer. You won't know if you don't ask. We all know this stuff, but do they know about you? Having it in stock is not enough; they have to know you want to sell it to them. Ask for the business.

3. Do you have a product or service that is unique in town? A second set of customers coming to you for those products will increase your hardware store volume as well. We have Budget Truck Rental and homebrewing supplies. Each counts as its own business, yet adds to the hardware store as well. Consider everything— pet grooming to Post Office. If it's something people have to go out to find, they will accidentally find your hardware store as well. Customers will tell each other about a unique product or service that they found at your store more readily than discussing ordinary nuts and bolts.

4. Are most of your middle-of-the-day customers women? If not, why not? After your contractor customers are on the job site, your store should be full of women. If women don't verbally compliment your store, they don't like it. If you don't hear , " I love coming here", they don't. Find out why.

5. Are you the best salesman for your business? Do you go to community events? Interact with the Rotary, Chamber of Commerce, school functions? Can you go into every business in town and they know you by name? Do you go to school music concerts, or local Little League or high school football games? Or are you a grumpy store owner waiting for business to come to you?

6. How is your Spanish? Like it or not, especially here in the rich, white Northeast, the hard work is being done by Hispanics. Get some Spanish-speaking employees, and take lessons yourself.

Your business depends on Spanish-speaking clientele. I speak Spanish (sort of) with five to ten customers every weekday. All are contractors or contractor employees. My Spanish-speaking employee gives me lessons. Our town's average household income is way over $100,000, and is mostly white, non-Hispanic, but my morning-going-to-work customers are often Hispanic. In my area, Korean would help too, but I'm not that good.

7. Do you spend some time with your customers and on the sales floor most every day? Walk them out to the car. Hang out in the parking lot. I find out more casual information outside, loading their car, then I do in the store. Read their bumper stickers and find some commonality.

Fifteen years ago I took a large chrome-plated bolt with a bright orange Karp's Hardware sticker to every gas/service station around here. I got the bolts surplus for pennies. We still have mechanics in the town that have that bolt sitting on top of their tool box. They use it like a magnetic business card stuck to a fridge. They call us for odd items and still tell us they took the number off the bolt.

The points are simple. We all need to do them; it doesn't need to cost a lot of money, but it won't do itself."

No one could have said it better!

CPSIA information can be obtained
at www.ICGtesting.com
Printed in the USA
FFHW01n1339200718
47502565-50838FF